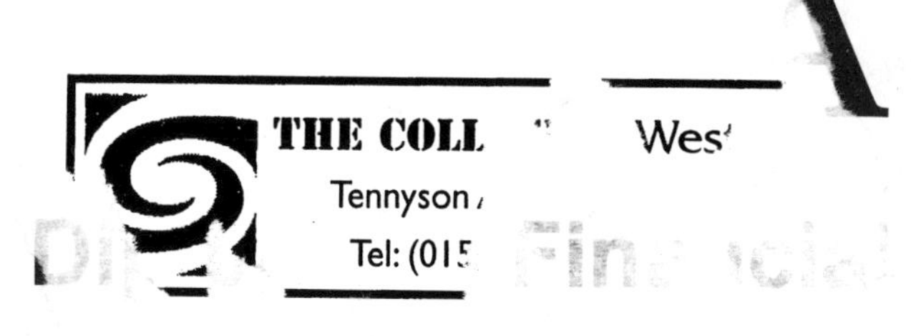

Practice & Revision Kit
Module B

Subject Area 4
Risk Management

This Practice & Revision Kit

BPP is the **official provider** of training materials for the ACCA's DipFM qualification.

In this November 2001 first edition

- Bank of multiple choice questions for each syllabus area
- Bank of practice questions and suggested answers for each syllabus area
- Mock exam (the Pilot Paper published by the ACCA with answers prepared by BPP)

FOR EXAMS IN 2002

BPP Publishing
December 2001

First edition December 2001

ISBN 0 7517 1707 X

British Library Cataloguing-in-Publication Data
A catalogue record for this book
is available from the British Library

Published by

BPP Publishing Limited
Aldine House, Aldine Place
London W12 8AW

www.bpp.com

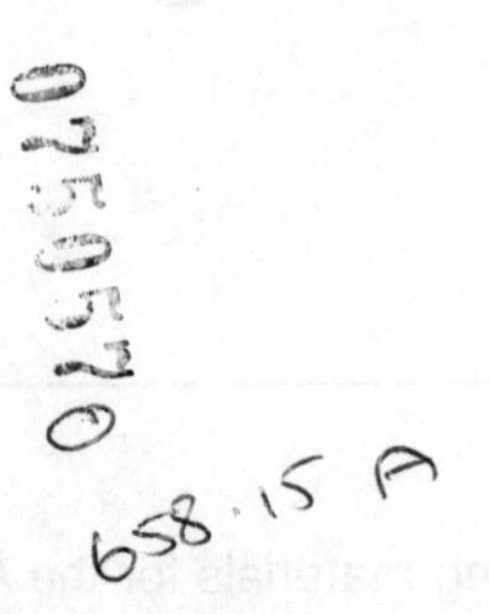

We are grateful to the Association of Chartered Certified Accountants for permission to reproduce the syllabus, the pilot paper and past examination questions of which the Association holds the copyright.

HOW TO USE THIS PRACTICE & REVISION KIT

Aim of this Practice & Revision Kit

To provide the practice to help you succeed in the examination for Subject Area 4, *Risk Management*

To pass the examination you need a thorough understanding in all areas covered by the syllabus and study guide.

Recommended approach

- Make sure you are able to answer questions on **everything** specified by the syllabus and study guide.
- Once you have completed all of the questions in the body of this Practice & Revision Kit, you should attempt the **MOCK EXAM** under examination conditions. Check your answers against our answers to find out how well you did.

This approach is only a suggestion. You or your college may well adapt it to suit your needs.

Remember this is a **practical** course.

- Try to relate the material to your experience in the workplace or any other work experience you may have had.
- Try to relate the technical content to Subject Area 3 of Module B, and if you have already studied it, to Module A.

SYLLABUS

Aim

There are two specific aims associated with this paper:

- To achieve a sound appreciation of the theory and practical aspects of corporate governance
- To develop an understanding of the main theories and frameworks associated with the management of both financial and non-financial risk

Objectives

On completion of this paper candidates should be able to

- Explain the drivers behind an organisation's appetite and consequent policy for managing risk
- Identify the main types of financial risk and evaluate the mechanisms available for managing exposure to them
- Discuss the various tools and techniques for identifying, measuring and communicating risk
- Discuss the importance of internal control in the management of risk
- Describe the various frameworks and codes enshrining good governance practice
- Explain the role of individuals and committees in implementing and reporting on good governance

POSITION WITHIN THE SYLLABUS

Candidates are expected to have a good knowledge of the issues underpinning financial strategy from subject area 3. Knowledge from subject areas 1 and 2 will be helpful, but not essential.

SYLLABUS CONTENT

1 **General risk management**

(a) Risk policy

(i) identification of risks

(ii) appetite for risk

(iii) management style

(b) Risk audit and risk mapping

(c) Reporting of risk management

2 **Management of Financial Risk**

(a) Defining and measuring financial risk

(b) Insurance

(c) Evaluation of the main types of financial risk including:

(i) foreign exchange risk

(ii) interest rate risk

(iii) credit risk

(iv) gearing

(v) cash flow

(d) Evaluation of the use of debt and equity

(i) cost of debt

(ii) cost of equity

(iii) WACC

(iv) Capital Asset Pricing Model

(e) Optimal Capital Structure

(f) Dividend policy

(i) influences on dividend policy

(ii) impact of dividends on company value

(g) Treasury Management

(i) business risk

(ii) market risk

(iii) responsibilities

(h) Definition and uses of derivatives including

(i) futures

(ii) options

(iii) forwards

(iv) interest and currency swaps

(v) caps

(vi) collars and floors

(vii) securitisation

(viii) hedging and risk manipulation

3 **Corporate Governance**

(a) Theoretical perspectives on corporate governance

(i) triggers for the introduction of systematised corporate governance

- (ii) rationale for governance procedures
- (iii) stakeholders and shareholders

(b) Key governance frameworks, codes and systems including:
- (i) Greenbury Report
- (ii) Cadbury Report
- (iii) Hampel Report/The Combined Code
- (iv) Turnbull Report
- (v) ABI Guideline Principles
- (vi) OECD Principles of Corporate Governance

(c) Role of Executives in corporate governance

(d) Role of Non-executives in corporate governance

(e) Internal Control
- (i) internal audit
- (ii) The Audit Committee
- (iii) The Remuneration Committee

(f) Implementation of Corporate Governance
- (i) statutory requirements
- (ii) stakeholder/shareholder expectations
- (iii) best practice

(g) Reporting of corporate governance
- (i) statutory requirements
- (ii) internal reporting

KEY AREAS OF THE SYLLABUS

The key topics are:

- The key drivers determining a business' general attitude to risk
- The elements and impacts of financial and non-financial risk
- Techniques available to identify and quantify risk
- Practical issues impacting the business' ability to manage risk
- Rationale and mechanisms for the implementation of corporate governance
- Responsibility, accountability, and reporting.

THE EXAMINATION PAPER

The examination for each module will cover the two subject areas in that module. The examination for Module B will cover both 'Financial Strategy' (subject area 3) and 'Risk Management' (subject area 4) topics.

The structure of the examination for Module B will be as follows.

Section A

20 multiple choice questions (10 covering subject area 3 and 10 covering subject area 4) of 2 marks each.

Section B

3 written questions of 20 marks each - covering subject area 3.

Section C

3 written questions of 20 marks each - covering subject area 4.

Candidates will be required to attempt all questions in Section A, one question from Section B, one question from Section C and one final question from either Section B or C.

The time allowed will be 3 hours.

The pass mark for the examination is 50%.

HOW TO PASS MODULE B

Revising with this Kit

A confidence boost

To boost your morale and to give yourself a bit of confidence, **start** your practice and revision with a topic that you find **straightforward**.

Diagnosis

A bank of **multiple choice questions** is included for each syllabus area. Use these questions as a **diagnostic tool**: if you get lots of them wrong go back to your BPP Study Text and do some revision; if you get the majority of them right, move on to any of the **practice questions** included for the syllabus area. These will provide you with a firm foundation from which to attempt the exam. The more questions you do, the more likely you are to pass the exam.

No cheating

Produce **full answers** under **timed conditions**; practising exam technique is just as important as recalling knowledge. Don't cheat by looking at the answer. Look back at your notes or at your BPP Study Text instead. Produce answer plans if you are running short of time.

Imagine you're the marker

It's a good idea to actually **mark your answers**. Don't be tempted to give yourself marks for what you meant to put down, or what you would have put down if you had time. And don't get despondent if you didn't do very well. Use the question and suggested answer to learn from your mistakes.

Trial run for the big day

Then, when you think you can successfully answer questions on the whole syllabus, attempt the **mock exam** at the end of the Kit. You will get the most benefit by sitting it under strict exam conditions, so that you gain experience of the four vital exam processes.

- Selecting questions
- Deciding on the order in which to attempt them
- Managing your time
- Producing answers

Tackling multiple choice questions

Of the total marks available for this paper, multiple choice questions comprise 20 per cent.

The multiple choice questions (MCQs) in your exam contain four possible answers. You have to **choose the option that best answers the question**. The three incorrect options are called distracters. There is a skill in answering MCQs quickly and correctly. By practising MCQs you can develop this skill, giving you a better chance of passing the exam.

You may wish to follow the approach outlined below, or you may prefer to adapt it.

Step 1. Skim read all the MCQs and identify what appear to be the easier questions.

Step 2. Attempt each question - **starting with the easier questions** identified in Step 1. Read the question thoroughly. You may prefer to work out the answer before looking at the options, or you may prefer to look at the options at the beginning. Adopt the method that works best for you.

Step 3. Read the four options and see if one matches your own answer. Be careful with numerical questions, as the distracters are designed to match answers that incorporate common errors. Check that your calculation is correct. Have you followed the requirement exactly? Have you included every stage of the calculation?

Step 4. You may find that none of the options matches your answer.

- Re-read the question to ensure that you understand it and are answering the requirement
- Eliminate any obviously wrong answers
- Consider which of the remaining answers is the most likely to be correct and select the option

Step 5. If you are still unsure make a note and continue to the next question. You have an average 3.6 minutes per multiple choice question. Some questions will take you longer to answer than others. Try to reduce the average time per question, to allow yourself to revisit problem questions at the end of the exam.

Step 6. Revisit unanswered questions. When you come back to a question after a break you often find you are able to answer it correctly straight away. If you are still unsure have a guess. You are not penalised for incorrect answers, so **never leave a question unanswered!**

Multiple choice questions

GENERAL RISK MANAGEMENT

Questions 1 to 7 cover general risk management, the subject of Part A of the BPP Study Text for Risk Management.

1 Risk mapping is a technique for assessing the severity of a risk and the probability or frequency of its likely occurrence. For what type of risk would it probably be most appropriate to take out an insurance policy from an insurance company?

A Severity high, frequency high
B Severity high, frequency low
C Severity low, frequency low
D Severity low, frequency high

2 A bank has assessed that there is only a 5% probability that the losses on its portfolio of assets will exceed £250 million. Which technique of risk management has the bank applied in reaching this analysis?

A Value at Risk
B Sensitivity analysis
C The Black-Scholes model
D Risk audit

3 What is the name given to a review by an organisation of all its risks?

A Risk mapping
B Risk management
C Risk assessment
D Risk audit

4 Which of the following definitions best describes risk aversion?

A Avoiding risks by refusing to invest in high-risk projects or investments

B Trying to reduce or minimise risks through risk management.

C Avoiding investments where the risk is high if an investment offering the same return for less risk is available

D Investing in projects offering the highest expected value of net present value

5 The most common measure of risk used to evaluate the risk/return trade-off is:

A Liquidity
B Probability of default
C Standard deviation of expected returns
D Probability of making a loss

6 A company is considering four projects which are mutually exclusive owing to a shortage of investment funds. For each project, it has estimated the internal rate of return, and calculated a measure of risk, based on probability analysis. The risk/return profile of each investment is as follows.

Project	*Return*	*Risk*
	%	%
W	18	6
X	17	7
Y	16	6
Z	18	7

If the company's board of directors is risk-averse in its project selection, which of these projects would it select?

A Project W
B Project X
C Project Y
D Project Z

7 A company is considering four mutually-exclusive investments, for which the expected internal rate of return and the expected risk (measured as a standard deviation of the expected return, based on estimated probabilities of different outcomes) are as follows:

Project	*Return*	*Risk*
	%	%
W	16	6
X	17	5
Y	18	7
Z	19	8

If the company's board of directors is risk-averse in its project selection, which of these projects would it **not** select?

A Project W
B Project X
C Project Y
D Project Z

If you struggled with these multiple choice questions, go back to your BPP Study Text for this paper and revise Chapter 1 before you tackle the written questions on general risk management.

MANAGEMENT OF FINANCIAL RISK

Questions 8 to 15 cover management of financial risk, the subject of Part B of the BPP Study Text for Risk Management.

8 Which of the following is the lowest investment grade in the Moody's system of credit ratings for bonds?

A Baa
B Ba
C B
D BBB

9 The current spot rate for the Singapore dollar against sterling is £1 = Sing $2.45. If Singapore experiences inflation at 2% each year over the next two years, and if the UK experiences inflation at 5% each year over the same period, what movements in the exchange rate should we expect in that time?

A Sterling will appreciate by about 3%
B Sterling will appreciate by about 6%
C Sterling will depreciate by about 3%
D Sterling will depreciate by about 6%

10 Which of the following risks is **not** associated with high financial gearing?

A Greater volatility in earnings
B Greater risk of inability to redeem debts
C Greater risk of inability to meet interest payment obligations
D Greater volatility in operating profit

11 A company is financed by a mixture of debt and equity. It has 50 million shares in issue, with a market value of £150 million. It also has £100 million of 8% debt capital, valued at par. The company expects to achieve earnings per share for the year of 14p. The rate of corporation tax is 30%.

What would be the percentage increase in EPS arising from an increase of 10% in operating profit?

A 8.1%
B 12.6%
C 15%
D 18%

12 What is meant by structural hedging?

A Trying to ensure as far as possible that a company has matching amounts of assets and liabilities in any currency, so as to reduce currency exposures

B Using the financial derivatives markets to hedge exposures to financial risks

C Managing the financial gearing of the company, to ensure that the company is always in a position to meet its debt payment obligations and have scope for further borrowing if needed

D Carrying out an annual review of the organisation's risks, and planning a risk management strategy to deal with them

13 What term is used to describe an organisation's exposures to the effect of changes in currency exchange rates on its international competitiveness?

A Translation exposures
B Transaction exposures
C Economic exposures
D Structural exposures

14 The following cash flows have been estimated for a capital expenditure project.

Cost of equipment (year 0)	£100,000
Revenues (years 1 – 5)	£50,000 each year
Running costs (years 1 – 5)	£20,000 each year
Project duration	5 years
Cost of capital	10%

The NPV of the project is + £13,700.

Discount factors at 10%

Year	*Factor*
1	0.90
2	0.82
3	0.75
4	0.68
5	0.62
1 – 5	3.79

Which of the following variables is most sensitive with regard to the overall financial viability of the project?

A Capital expenditure
B Revenues
C Running costs
D Project duration

15 The following cash flows have been estimated for a capital expenditure project.

Cost of equipment (year 0)	£200,000
Revenues (years 1 – 5)	£200,000 each year
Running costs (years 1 – 5)	£120,000 each year
Project duration	5 years
Cost of capital	12%

Discount factors at 12%

Year	*Factor*
1	0.89
2	0.80
3	0.71
4	0.64
5	0.57
1 – 5	3.61

Which of the following variables is least sensitive with regard to the overall financial viability of the project?

A Capital expenditure
B Revenues
C Running costs
D Project duration

If you struggled with these multiple choice questions, go back to your BPP Study Text for this paper and revise Chapters 2 to 4 before you tackle the written questions on management of financial risk.

DEBT AND EQUITY, OPTIMAL CAPITAL STRUCTURE, DIVIDEND POLICY

Questions 16 to 27 cover debt and equity, optimal capital structure, dividend policy, included in Part B of the BPP Study Text for Risk Management.

16 A company's shares have a beta of 0.85. The risk-free rate of return is 3.5% and the expected market return is 6%. What is the expected return on the company's shares?

A 5.1%
B 5.625%
C 8.125%
D 8.6%

17 A company's shares have an alpha value of +2.0% for a given period. The market rate of return for the period is 6% and the beta of the share is 1.2. If the risk-free rate of return is 4%, what was the return on the share?

A 4.4%
B 6.4%
C 8.4%
D 10.4%

18 Shares in Hat plc have a beta of 0.8. The risk-free return is 3%. Due to adverse stock market conditions, the average market return is – 5%. What would be the expected return on Hat shares?

A - 3.4%
B - 4.0%
C - 6.4%
D + 1.4%

19 Risk which is specific to a particular share is called:

A Systematic risk
B Market risk
C Unsystematic risk
D Undiversifiable risk

20 A share has a beta of zero, the risk-free rate of return is 3% and the market premium for risk is 6%. What is the required return on the share?

A 0%
B 3%
C 6%
D 9%

21 Four companies are identical in all respects, except for their capital structures, which are as follows.

	W plc	*X plc*	*Y plc*	*Z plc*
Equity as a proportion of total market capitalisation	95%	80%	50%	40%
Debt as a proportion of total market capitalisation	5%	20%	50%	60%

The beta value of the equity shares of X plc is 0.90 and the beta of the equity of Z plc is 1.57.

Within which range will the beta values of the equity of W plc and Y plc lie?

A The beta of W plc is above 1.57 and the beta of Y plc is below 0.90
B The beta of W plc and the beta of Y plc are both below 0.90
C The beta of W plc is above 1.57 and the beta of Y plc is within the range 0.90 to 1.57
D The beta of W plc is below 0.90 and the beta of Y plc is within the range 0.90 to 1.57

22 A company has issued share capital with a current market capitalisation of £80 million. It has also issued £50 million of 7% bonds with a current market value of 94.00. The after-tax cost of the bonds is 5.25%. The expected market return is 9%, the risk-free interest rate is 5% and the beta factor for the company's equity is 1.10.

What is the company's weighted average cost of capital?

A 7.8%
B 7.9%
C 8.7%
D 8.8%

23 What is indicated by a dividend cover of less than 1?

A The company is insolvent

B The dividend payment has been partly satisfied by accumulated profits

C The company has exhausted its distributable reserves

D The company has made substantial exceptional profits during the year that have been paid out as dividends

24 What is the residual theory of dividend policy?

A That companies should pursue a policy of smoothing dividends from one year to the next, and reinvest only those profits that are not needed to maintain the dividend payments

B That dividends should act as a signal to the market, and should be used by a company to indicate to investors its likely future prospects

C That companies should invest profits in all available projects with a positive net present value, and pay out as dividend only what profits are left over

D That companies should have a long-run aim of paying out a fixed proportion of earnings as dividends, and only use what is left to re-invest long-term in the company

25 Strike plc has just made profits after tax of £4 million. Its cost of capital is 10%, and it can re-invest retained profits to earn returns of 10% per annum. Which of the following dividend policies would maximise the total value of the company's equity, assuming that the dividend growth model of share valuation is valid?

Policy	*Proportion of profits re-invested*
1	25%
2	50%
3	75%

A Policy 1 will maximise shareholder value
B Policy 2 will maximise shareholder value
C Policy 3 will maximise shareholder value
D Shareholder value is unaffected by dividend policy

26 The cost of equity in an ungeared company is 12%. The cost of risk-free debt is 5%. According to Modigliani and Miller, what would be the cost of equity in a similar geared company which is 50% equity-financed and 50% debt-financed, assuming a corporation tax rate of 20%?

A 14.8%
B 15.5%
C 16.0%
D 17.6%

27 A plc and B plc are companies in the same industry, with the same business risk and operating characteristics. A plc is an all-equity company, with shares valued at £100 million. The annual profits of A plc are double those of B plc. Corporation tax is 30%. B plc is financed partly by 10% debt capital, which has a market value of £20 million. The value of A plc shares is thought to be at its equilibrium level.

According to Modigliani and Miller, what will be the equilibrium value of the equity shares of B plc?

A £36 million
B £56 million
C £86 million
D £106 million

If you struggled with these multiple choice questions, go back to your BPP Study Text for this paper and revise Chapters 5 to 8 before you tackle the written questions on cost of capital, capital structure and dividend policy.

TREASURY MANAGEMENT AND DERIVATIVES

Questions 28 to 57 cover treasury management and derivatives, included in Part B of the BPP Study Text for Risk Management.

28 An investor buys a put option on XYZ shares, with an exercise price of 250p. The option was bought for a premium of 10p. If the price on expiry of the option is 220p, what is the gain or loss made by the investor?

A 10p gain
B 20p gain
C 30p gain
D 10p loss

29 The Canadian dollar/Swiss franc (C$/SFr) exchange rate is quoted three months forward at 1.0185 – 1.0195. What would it cost a company to sell SFr 1,000,000 three months forward at the quoted rate?

A C$1,019,500
B C$1,018,500
C C$981,836
D C$980,873

30 A eurodollar bank account yields 5% per annum. A company places £100,000 on deposit for three months at an exchange rate of £1 = $1.43, and sells the proceeds forward for that period at $1.40. What is the return on investment for the three-month period?

A 1.25%
B 1.28%
C 3.42%
D 7.25%

31 The spot sterling/Japanese yen exchange rate is quoted at 172.05 – 172.15. The three month forward rate is quoted as 165 – 162 premium. This implies that:

A UK three-month interest rates are about 0.9% per annum lower than Japanese three-month rates

B UK three-month interest rates are about 3.8% per annum lower than Japanese three-month rates

C UK three-month interest rates are about 0.9% per annum higher than Japanese three-month rates

D UK three-month interest rates are about 3.8% higher than Japanese three-month rates

32 The sterling/US dollar spot rate is 1.4770 – 1.4860 and the forward rate is quoted as 0.36 – 0.35 cents premium. At what forward rate will the bank sell US dollars?

A 1.4734
B 1.4806
C 1.4825
D 1.4895

33 As company treasurer, you are depositing cash (sterling) in August, and are worried that interest rates will soon fall. Which of the following would be an appropriate hedging transaction?

A Sell June short sterling futures
B Sell September short sterling futures
C Buy June short sterling futures
D Buy September short sterling futures

34 What is the maximum liability of the writer of a put option?

A Unlimited
B Zero
C Exercise price – Premium
D Exercise price + Premium

35 The current spot rate for US dollar/South African rand (US$/R) is 8.7580 – 8.7600. The three-month forward rate is quoted as 0.0090 – 0.0100 discount. You wish to convert R5 million into US dollars in three months' time, and you intend to hedge the currency exposure with a forward exchange contract. How many US dollars will you receive in three months' time?

A $570,125
B $570,321
C $571,429
D $571,494

36 A company holds shares, which it believes will soon fall in price, in another listed company. It wishes to hold on to the shares as a strategic investment, and to hedge the exposure to a price fall. Which of the following would be appropriate trades to hedge the market risk exposure?

I Buy call options on the shares
II Sell call options on the shares
III Buy put options on the shares
IV Sell put options on the shares

A Trades I and III
B Trades I and IV
C Trades II and III
D Trades II and IV

37 What would be the impact on premiums for at-the-money options if the price volatility of the underlying item were to increase?

A Call premiums would go up, and put premiums would go down
B Call premiums would go down, and put premiums would go up
C Call and put premiums would both go up
D Call and put premiums would both go down

38 Variation margin is called on all futures positions. What does variation margin represent?

A The worst probable day loss on a position
B The actual profit or loss on a position each day
C The expected profit or loss on a position each day
D Two-thirds of the initial margin

39 A US company has made a sale to a customer in Germany for €5 million, with payment due in two months. How could the company hedge its exchange rate exposure during this period using currency futures or options on currency futures?

A Buy euro futures or buy call options on euro futures
B Sell euro futures or buy call options on euro futures
C Buy euro futures or buy put options on euro futures
D Sell euro futures or buy put options on euro futures

40 A company's treasurer has authority to speculate in stock options. He believes the stock market is about to become more volatile, but is not sure whether it will move up or down. He buys a put for January at 5000, a premium of 75, and buys a call for January at 5000 for 55, when the underlying stock market index is 4980. To make a profit on his options trades at expiry, the stock market index would have to lie outside the range:

A 4850 – 5110
B 4870 – 5130
C 4925 – 5055
D 4905 – 5035

41 Three-month sterling March futures are quoted on LIFFE at 94.00. Call options on three-month sterling March futures at 93.50 are quoted at 0.56. This premium of 0.56 represents:

A 0.56 intrinsic value
B 0.56 time value
C 0.50 intrinsic value and 0.06 time value
D 0.06 intrinsic value and 0.50 time value

42 What is the time value of a September put option at a strike price of 101 which has 87 days remaining to expiry and a premium of 4.17, when the price of the underlying item is 103.50?

A 4.17
B 2.50
C 1.67
D 0

43 A company sold three three-month sterling futures at 95.79 and closed the position by buying three contracts at 94.91. The contract size is £500,000 and a tick is one basis point (one hundredth of one per cent, or 0.0001). What is the profit on the transactions?

A £1,100
B £3,300
C £4,400
D £13,200

44 If you were to buy a 100 put for a premium of 12, what would be your maximum possible profit?

A Unlimited
B 100
C 88
D 12

45 You are expecting to borrow $50 million in five months' time, for a period of six months. Which of the following instruments would enable you to hedge against the risk of an increase in interest rates in the next five months?

A Forward exchange rate
B Interest rate cap
C FRA
D Buying an interest rate put option over the counter

46 A company wants to create a hedge against the risk of a rise in six-month interest rates during the next five months, when the interest rate on its £8 million floating rate bank loan will be re-set. Which of the following would provide a suitable hedge?

A Buy a 5 v 11 FRA
B Buy a 6 v 11 FRA
C Sell a 5 v 11 FRA
D Sell a 6 v 11 FRA

47 A company buys a $10 million 6 v 9 FRA on 12 February for settlement on 12 August, based on a maturity date of 12 November. The contract period is 92 days and US money market interest is calculated on the basis of actual interest days and a 360-day year. The FRA rate is 6.8% and the three-month LIBOR settlement rate at fixing is 7.25%.

What is the amount payable at settlement on 12 August?

A The company will receive £11,290.86 from the bank
B The company will receive £11,303.57 from the bank
C The company will receive £11,500 from the bank
D The company will pay £11,290.86 to the bank

48 A company can borrow at 125 basis points above LIBOR. It wants to fix the interest rate for a three-month loan, starting in four months' time. A bank has quoted the following FRA rates:

	Bid	*Offer*
3 v 7	5.68	5.64
4 v 7	5.73	5.69

What will be the effective borrowing rate secured by the company through its purchase of an FRA?

A 6.89%
B 6.91%
C 6.93%
D 6.98%

49 A company has a floating rate loan of £5 million with four years remaining to maturity, on which it pays interest of LIBOR plus 75 basis points, but it would prefer to pay a fixed rate of interest on this loan amount. It therefore arranges a 'plain vanilla' four-year interest rate swap. The bank's rates for a four-year swap are 5.20% - 5.25%. What is the effective net interest rate that the company will pay, as a result of arranging the swap?

A 4.45%
B 4.50%
C 5.95%
D 6.00%

50 A company can borrow at a fixed rate by issuing five-year bonds at 7.4% or can borrow at a variable rate of LIBOR + 100 basis points. It has been quoted rates of 6.70% - 6.75% for a five-year plain vanilla swap. The company wants to borrow at a floating rate of interest. How much would it save by borrowing fixed and arranging a swap, compared with issuing bonds?

A 0.30%
B 0.35%
C 0.70%
D It would be cheaper to issue bonds

51 A company has a three-year variable rate loan of £6 million on which it pays three-month LIBOR plus 100 basis points. It would prefer to borrow at a fixed rate, and mostly in euros. A bank quotes a fixed rate of 3.25% for the euro in a cross-currency swap. The rate of exchange for the swap would be (€/£) 0.6667, i.e. €0.6667 per £1. What will be the payments in the swap?

A The company will pay 3.25% on €10 million and receive interest on £6 million at LIBOR, and at maturity the company will pay €10 million in exchange for receiving £6 million.

B The company will pay 3.25% on €10 million and receive interest on £6 million at LIBOR, and at maturity the company will pay £6 million in exchange for receiving €10 million.

C The company will receive 3.25% on €10 million and pay interest on £6 million at LIBOR, and at maturity the company will pay €10 million in exchange for receiving £6 million.

D The company will receive 3.25% on €10 million and pay interest on £6 million at LIBOR, and at maturity the company will pay £6 million in exchange for receiving €10 million.

52 Swaps could be used for a number of different purposes. Which of the following would not be a reason for entering a swap transaction?

A To switch net interest obligations out of one currency and into another currency.

B To benefit from favourable interest changes during the term of the swap

C To reduce net borrowing costs through credit arbitrage

D To alter the mix of fixed and floating rate debt obligations in the organisation's debt structure.

53 A company has arranged a three-year variable rate loan at LIBOR plus 50 basis points. It has also arranged an interest rate collar which fixes a maximum effective borrowing cost for the company of 7.5% and a minimum effective borrowing cost of 6.5%. What does the collar consist of?

A With the collar, the company has bought a series of consecutive interest rate call options at a strike price of 7% and sold a matching series of put options at 6%.

B With the collar, the company has bought a series of consecutive interest rate call options at a strike price of 7% and bought a matching series of put options at 6%.

C With the collar, the company has bought a series of consecutive interest rate call options at a strike price of 7% and sold a matching series of put options at 7%.

D With the collar, the company has bought a series of consecutive interest rate call options at a strike price of 7% and bought a matching series of put options at 7%.

54 A company has arranged an interest rate cap, with a strike rate of 7%, for a notional principal amount of £10 million. The benchmark interest rate is six-month LIBOR. The fixing rate for LIBOR, for two consecutive interest periods, was as follows:

Period	*LIBOR rate*	*Number of days in period*
1	6.50%	181
2	7.50%	184

What compensation payments are payable in each period?

A Period 1: Bank pays company £24,020. Period 2: no payment
B Period 1: Bank pays company £24,795. Period 2: no payment
C Period 1: no payment. Period 2: Bank pays company £24,287
D Period 2: no payment. Period 2: Bank pays company £25,205

55 Calculate the forward per annum premium or discount from the following information.

Spot exchange rate for euro/Hungarian forint = 259.25

Three month forward rate, euro/forint = 263.83

A The forint is at a premium of 1.8% p.a. to the euro.
B The forint is at a premium of 7.1% p.a. to the euro
C The forint is at a discount of 1.8% p.a. to the euro
D The forint is at a discount of 7.1% p.a. to the euro

56 In the Black-Scholes model for calculating the value of an option, there are several variables influencing the option price. With which of the following factors does the price of a call option vary inversely, so that the option price will go down as the value of the factor rises?

A Volatility in the price of the underlying item
B The current price of the underlying item
C The exercise price of the option
D The time to expiry of the option

57 A corporate treasurer wishes to invest surplus cash of the company in gilts, but wants to minimise the risk of losses through rising interest rates. Which of the following categories of gilts would be best-suited for his purpose?

A Long-dated gilts with a low coupon
B Long-dated gilts with a high coupon
C Short-dated gilts with a low coupon
D Short-dated gilts with a high coupon

> If you struggled with these multiple choice questions, go back to your BPP Study Text for this paper and revise Chapters 9 to 14 before you tackle the written questions on treasury management and derivatives.

CORPORATE GOVERNANCE

Questions 58 to 66 cover corporate governance, the subject of Part C of the BPP Study Text for Risk Management.

58 What is the minimum number of non-executive directors recommended for the board of directors of a listed company by the Combined Code?

A Two
B Three
C At least one quarter of the board
D At least one third of the board

59 The Combined Code recommends that non-executive directors should make up the membership of certain sub-committees of the board of directors of a listed company. Which of the following committees is **not** specified by the Code as a committee that should be made up of non-executive directors?

A Risk committee
B Audit committee
C Remuneration committee
D Nominations committee

60 Which of the following guidelines has been issued to its members by the ABI?

A The most appropriate long-term share incentive scheme for senior executives should be based on Total Shareholder Return as a measure of performance

B Share options should be issued to senior executives infrequently, but in sufficiently large amounts to provide an incentive for better performance

C Shareholders should restrict their approval for the quantity of shares that a board of directors can issue without a rights issue to 2.5% within any rolling two-year period

D Shareholders should give positive support to the board of directors, unless there is a good reason for not doing so

61 Which of the following is not a recommendation of the Turnbull report for listed companies?

A All companies should have in place a robust system of internal control

B Risks facing the business should be reviewed regularly by senior management

C All companies should have an internal audit department, which should review the system of controls at least every two years

D Risk management is the collective responsibility of the board of directors, although some aspects of the work can be delegated

62 The OECD principles of corporate governance are dividend into five categories. One of these is the equitable treatment of shareholders. Which of the following principles comes within this category?

A The directors should disclose to shareholders any material interest they have in transactions affecting the company

B The equity shareholders should have the right to elect the members of the board of directors

C Where a stakeholder's rights are protected by law, the stakeholder should have an opportunity to obtain effective redress for any violation of those rights

D Anti-takeover devices should not be used to shield management from accountability

63 Which of the following would not be a breach of the OECD principles?

A An article in the company's constitution whereby the voting rights of any shareholder with more than 30% of the equity shares should be restricted to just 20%

B A refusal by the board of directors to appoint non-executive directors

C Calling a general meeting of the company at short notice, giving foreign shareholders no time to arrange attendance or proxy voting

D Using as the external auditor an individual or firm of accountants that is not independent of the company

64 What is the purpose of a nominations committee of the board of directors?

A To nominate the directors who should stand for re-election at each annual general meeting of the company

B To put forward nominations for new appointments to the board

C To decide whether to accept nominations for new appointments to the board, put forward by the chairman or the chief executive officer

D To review nominations for appointments to senior executive posts and the position of company secretary

65 Which of the following is a requirement of the Combined Code?

A There should be at least four formal board meetings each year

B The board should use the annual general meeting to communicate with private investors in the company

C Non-executive directors should attend at least one half of the formal board meetings each year

D When the roles of chairman and chief executive officer are separated, there is no requirement for a senior non-executive director

66 Which report in the UK introduced the recommendation that a remuneration report should be published in or with the annual report and accounts of listed companies?

A Cadbury report
B Greenbury report
C Hampel report
D Turnbull report

> If you struggled with these multiple choice questions, go back to your BPP Study Text for this paper and revise Chapters 15 to 17 before you tackle the written questions on corporate governance.

Practice questions

GENERAL RISK MANAGEMENT AND FINANCIAL RISK

Questions 1 to 4 cover general risk management and financial risk, the subject of Chapters 1 and 2 of the BPP Study Text for Risk Management.

1 STRUCTURED APPROACH

A structured approach to risk management will involve the identification and assessment of risks, risk profiling and quantification, and deciding on what measures or policies to adopt for risk management.

Required

Explain how a structured approach to risk management might be taken by an international airline company. In your explanation, you should:

(a) suggest how risks might be categorised by the company
(b) explain the difference between financial and non-financial risk, and
(c) explain the relevance of materiality to risk assessment.

(20 marks)

2 PROJECT RISK

(a) When an organisation undertakes a major investment project, it takes on project risk. The risk in a project comes from various sources, and includes:

(i) project specific risk
(ii) competitive risk
(iii) industry-specific risk
(iv) international risk, and
(v) market risk.

Describe what is meant by each of these types of risk. (10 marks)

(b) The decision by a company to invest in a project, or the decision by an investor to invest in the shares of a company, are based on an assessment of risk and returns. Some companies and investors have a different attitude to risk from others.

Required

(i) What is meant by risk and returns for an investment?

(ii) What is the difference between risk-aversion and risk-seeking, and how might these different attitudes to risk affect an investment decision? (10 marks)

(20 marks)

3 MEASURING RISK

(a) What is the difference between financial and non-financial risk? (3 marks)

(b) Describe the different ways that could be used for measuring risk in a project investment, including sensitivity analysis. (6 marks)

(c) Sternum plc is considering a two-year project to make and sell a single product. It has been estimated that the product will sell for £10 per unit, and will have a variable cost of £4 per unit. Directly attributable annual fixed costs would be £150,000 for any volume of annual production.

The marketing department has produced the following estimates of sales each year.

Year 1	*Units sold*	*Probability*
	50,000	0.8
	70,000	0.2

Year 2	*Units sold in year 2*	*Probability*
Units sold in year 1		
50,000	20,000	0.4
50,000	40,000	0.6
Units sold in year 1		
70,000	50,000	0.3
70,000	60,000	0.7

The initial cost of the investment would be £200,000 at the start of the project.

Ignore taxation and inflation, and ignore any working capital investment.

The company has a cost of capital of 10%.

Year	*Discount factor at 10%*
1	0.91
2	0.83

Required

(i) What is the expected net present value of the project?

(ii) By how much would the initial capital expenditure need to exceed the estimate before the expected value of the project became negative?

(iii) By how much would the expected sales volume need to fall short of the estimate before the expected value of the project became negative?

(iv) Describe an alternative approach to risk assessment in this example, other than sensitivity analysis. **(11 marks)**

(20 marks)

4 TREASURER

You have recently been appointed as deputy treasurer of an international company. Your chief executive has asked you to write a brief report to the non-executive directors, to explain to them various aspects of financial risk.

Required

Prepare the report that your chief executive has requested. In your report, you should cover the following issues:

(a) the meaning and nature of financial risk (2 marks)

(b) the meaning of currency risk, and the nature of transaction exposures and economic exposures (5 marks)

(c) the meaning of interest rate risk (3 marks)

(d) the meaning of the term structure of interest rates and its relevance to risk management (5 marks)

(e) the meaning of credit risk, with suggestions for how it should be managed (2 marks)

(f) the meaning of free cash flow, and its significance for risk management. (3 marks)

(20 marks)

COST OF CAPITAL AND CAPITAL STRUCTURE

Questions 5 to 9 cover cost of capital and capital structure, included in Part B of the BPP Study Text for Risk Management.

5 KILTER PLC

Kilter plc is a food manufacturer which has the following long-term capital structure.

	£
£1 ordinary shares (fully paid)	25,000,000
Share premium account	10,000,000
Retained profit	20,000,000
8% preference shares	6,000,000
10% debentures (secured)	26,000,000
	87,000,000

The directors of the company want to raise additional long-term capital by issuing either ordinary shares or obtaining more debt capital. One director, who supports the debt financing option, believes that although extra debt capital would increase the company's gearing, it would reduce the overall cost of capital.

Required

(a) Explain briefly the rationale behind wanting to reduce the company's overall cost of capital. (3 marks)

(b) Discuss the arguments for and against the view that the company's overall cost of capital can be reduced in this way. The views of Modigliani and Miller should be discussed in answering this part of the question. (8 marks)

(c) Identify and discuss the major factors that will influence the amount of additional debt finance that Kilter plc will be able to raise. (9 marks)

(20 marks)

6 BLANK LIMITED

Blank Limited is a private limited company with intentions of obtaining a stock market listing in the near future. The company is wholly equity financed at present but the directors are considering a new capital structure prior to it becoming a listed company.

Blank Ltd operates in an industry where the average asset beta is 1.2. The company's business risk is estimated to be similar to that of the industry as a whole. The current level of earnings before interest and taxes is £400,000. This earnings level is expected to be maintained for the foreseeable future.

The rate of return on risk-less assets is at present 10% and the return on the market portfolio is 15%. These rates are post-tax and are expected to remain constant for the foreseeable future.

Blank Ltd is considering introducing debt into its capital structure by one of the following methods.

(a) £500,000 10% Debentures at par, secured on land and buildings of the company
(b) £1,000,000 12% Unsecured loan stock at par.

The company would use the money raised from the debt issuance to buy back and cancel equity shares.

The rate of corporation tax is expected to remain at 30% and interest on debt is tax deductible.

Required

(a) Calculate, for *each* of the *two* debt financing options:

(i) The values of equity *and* the total market value of the company
(ii) The debt/equity ratio
(iii) The cost of equity, assuming that all earnings are paid out as dividends. (10 marks)

(b) 'Capital structure can have no influence on the value of the firm.'

Discuss this statement and comment briefly on the practical factors that a company may take into account when determining capital structure. (10 marks)

(20 marks)

7 DRYSTONE PLC

The following is an extract from the balance sheet of Drystone plc at 30 June 20X3.

	£000
Ordinary shares of 50p each	5,200
Reserves	4,850
9% preference shares of £1 each	4,500
14% debentures	5,000
Total long-term funds	19,550

The ordinary shares are quoted at 80p. Assume that the market estimate of the next ordinary dividend is 4p, growing thereafter at 12% per annum indefinitely. The preference shares, which are irredeemable, are quoted at 72p and the debentures are quoted at par. Corporation tax is 30%.

Required

(a) Use the relevant data above to estimate the company's weighted average cost of capital (WACC), i.e. the return required by the providers of the three types of capital, using the respective market values as weighting factors. (8 marks)

(b) Explain how the capital asset pricing model would be used as an alternative method of estimating the cost of equity, indicating what information would be required and how it would be obtained. (8 marks)

(c) Assume that instead of raising £5 million of 14% debentures, the company had raised the equivalent amount in preference shares giving the same yield as the existing preference capital.

Calculate how Drystone plc's equity earnings would have been affected if the preference shares had been issued instead of the loan capital. (4 marks)

(20 marks)

8 PUMP AND FLOW

(a) Pump plc has annual earnings before interest and tax of £15 million. These earnings are expected to remain constant. The market price of the company's ordinary shares is 86 pence per share cum div and of debentures £104.17 per debenture ex interest. An interim dividend of six pence per share has been declared. Corporate tax is at the rate of 30% and all available earnings are distributed as dividends.

Pump's long-term capital structure is shown below.

	£000
Ordinary shares of 25p (nominal value)	12,500
Reserves	24,300
	36,800
16% debentures, redeemable 31.12.X4	24,000
	60,800

Required

Calculate the cost of capital of Pump plc according to the traditional theory of capital structure. Assume that it is now 31 December 20X1. (8 marks)

(b) Flow plc is an all equity company with an equilibrium market value of £32.5 million and a cost of capital of 18% per year. The company proposes to repurchase £5 million of equity and to replace it with 13% irredeemable loan stock.

Flow's earnings before interest and tax are expected to be constant for the foreseeable future. Corporate tax is at the rate of 30%. All profits are paid out as dividends.

Required

Using the assumptions of Modigliani and Miller explain and demonstrate how this change in capital structure will affect:

(i) the market value of the company's equity
(ii) the weighted average cost of capital
(iii) the cost of equity (7 marks)

(c) Explain any weaknesses of both the Modigliani and Miller theory and discuss how useful it might be in the determination of the appropriate capital structure for a company. (5 marks)

(20 marks)

Discount factors *Year*	*At 8%*	At 10%
1	0.93	0.91
2	0.86	0.83
3	0.79	0.75

9 NETRA AND BACKWOODS

(a) The finance director of Netra plc, a small UK listed company, wishes to estimate what impact the introduction of debt finance is likely to have on the company's overall cost of capital. The company is currently financed only by equity.

Netra plc

Summarised capital structure

	£000
Ordinary shares (25p nominal value)	500
Reserves	1,100
	1,600

The company's current share price is 420 pence, and up to £4 million of fixed-rate five-year debt could be raised at an interest rate of 10% per annum. The corporate tax rate is 30%.

Netra's current earnings before interest and tax are £2.5 million. These earnings are not expected to change significantly for the foreseeable future.

The company is considering raising either:

(1) £2 million in debt finance; or
(2) £4 million in debt finance.

In either case the debt finance will be used to repurchase ordinary shares.

Required

(i) Using Miller and Modigliani's model in a world with corporate tax, estimate the impact on Netra's cost of capital of raising:

(1) £2 million; or
(2) £4 million in debt finance

State clearly any assumptions that you make. (4 marks)

(ii) Briefly discuss whether or not the estimates produced in part (a) are likely to be accurate. (4 marks)

(b) Backwoods plc is a major international company with its head office in the UK, wanting to raise €150 million to establish a new production plant in the eastern region of Germany. Backwoods evaluates its investments using NPV, but is not sure what cost of capital to use in the discounting process for this project evaluation.

The company is also proposing to increase its equity finance in the near future for UK expansion, resulting overall in little change in the company's market-weighted capital gearing.

The summarised financial data for the company before the expansion are shown below.

Profit and loss account for the year ended 31 December 20X1

	£m
Turnover	1,984
Gross profit	432
Profit after tax	81
Dividends	37
Retained earnings	44

Balance sheet as at 31 December 20X1

	£m
Net fixed assets	846
Working capital	350
	1,196
Medium term and long term loans (see note below)	210
	986
Shareholders' funds	
Issued ordinary shares of £0.50 each nominal value	225
Reserves	761
	986

Note on borrowings

These include £75m 14% fixed rate bonds due to mature in five years time and redeemable at par. The current market price of these bonds is £120.00. Other medium and long-term loans are floating rate UK bank loans at LIBOR plus 1%.

Corporate rate tax may be assumed to be at the rate of 30%. The company's ordinary shares are currently trading at 376 pence.

The equity beta of Backwoods is estimated to be 1.18. The systematic risk of debt may be assumed to be zero. The risk free rate is 7.75% and market return 14.5%.

The estimated equity beta of the main German competitor in the same industry as the new proposed plant in the eastern region of Germany is 1.5, and the competitor's capital gearing is 35% equity and 65% debt by book values, and 60% equity and 40% debt by market values.

Required

Estimate the cost of capital that the company should use as the discount rate for its proposed investment in eastern Germany. State clearly any assumptions that you make.

(12 marks)

(20 marks)

DIVIDEND POLICY

Questions 10 to 13 cover dividend policy, included in Part B of the BPP Study Text for Risk Management.

10 DIVIDENDS

(a) It has been argued that the pattern of dividends paid to shareholders is irrelevant when valuing the shares of a company. Explain this argument. (6 marks)

(b) Evaluate the argument explained in (a) above. Include in your evaluation the implications of this argument for the financial management of a company. Also include in your evaluation two reasons why, in practice, the pattern of dividends paid to shareholders is usually considered by managers to be important. (10 marks)

(c) Briefly identify two factors relating to the financial aspects of a company which may, in practice, influence the level of dividends a company distributes to its shareholders

(4 marks)

(20 marks)

11 XYZ PLC

The table below shows earnings and dividends for XYZ plc over the past five years.

Year	*Net earnings per share*	*Net dividend per share*
	£	£
20X1	1.40	0.84
20X2	1.35	0.88
20X3	1.35	0.90
20X4	1.30	0.95
20X5	1.25	1.00

There are 10,000,000 shares in issue and most of them are owned by private investors. There is no debt in the capital structure.

The company has experienced difficult trading conditions over the past few years. In the current year, 20X6, net earnings are likely to be £10 million, which will be just sufficient to pay a maintained dividend of £1 per share.

Members of the board are considering a number of strategies for the company, some of which will have an impact on the company's future dividend policy.

The company's shareholders require a return of 15% on their investment.

Four options are being considered, as follows.

1. Pay out all earnings as dividends.

2. Pay a reduced dividend of 50% of earnings and retain the remaining 50% for future investment.

3. Pay a reduced dividend of 25% of earnings and retain the remaining 75% for future investment.

4. Retain all earnings for an aggressive expansion programme and pay no dividend at all.

The directors cannot agree on any of the four options discussed so far. Some of them prefer option (1) because they believe to do anything else would have an adverse impact on the

share price. Others favour either option (2) or option (3) because the company has identified some good investment opportunities and they believe one of these options would be in the best long-term interests of shareholders. An adventurous minority favours option (4) and thinks this will allow the company to take over a small competitor.

Required

(a) Comment on the company's dividend policy between 20X1 and 20X5 and on the possible consequences for earnings that this policy might have had. (6 marks)

(b) Using an appropriate valuation model, advise the directors of the share price for XYZ plc which might be expected immediately following the announcement of their decision if they pursued each of the four options. Make (and indicate) any realistic assumptions you think necessary to answer this question. Indicate how much of the return to shareholders will be provided by dividends, and how much will be provided by capital growth. (8 marks)

(c) Discuss the reliability you can place on the figures you have just produced and on the usefulness of this information to the company's directors. (6 marks)

(20 marks)

12 POSTER PLC

The following financial data relate to Poster plc.

Year	*Earnings per share*	*Net dividend per share*	*Share price*
	pence	pence	pence
20X1	42	17	252
20X2	46	18	184
20X3	51	20	255
20X4	55	22	275
20X5	62	25	372

'Now' is the end of 20X5.

Equity market analysts of a leading investment bank have recently re-evaluated the company's future prospects. The analysts estimate that Poster plc's earnings and dividends will grow at 25% for the next two years. Thereafter, earnings are likely to increase at a lower annual rate of 10%. If this reduction in earnings growth occurs, the analysts consider that the dividend payout ratio will be increased to 50%.

Poster plc is all-equity financed and has one million ordinary shares in issue.

The tax rate of 30% is not expected to change in the foreseeable future.

Required

(a) Calculate the estimated share price and P/E ratio which the analysts now expect for Poster plc, using the dividend valuation model, and comment briefly on the method of valuation you have just used. Assume a constant post-tax cost of capital of 18%. (12 marks)

(b) Comment on the dividend policy of Poster plc in recent years, and describe briefly *three* other dividend policies which Poster plc could consider. (8 marks)

(20 marks)

Discount factors at 18%

Year	*Factor*
0	1.00
1	0.85
2	0.72
3	0.61
4	0.52

13 SAND PLC

Sand plc is a large international company with widespread interests in advertising, media and various media consultancy activities. In recent years the company has achieved growth, in real terms, of 15% in annual earnings and 12% in dividend payments. The company is likely to have a substantial cash surplus in the coming year, but a number of investment opportunities are being considered for the subsequent two years. The senior managers of the company are reviewing their likely funding requirements for the next two to three years and the possible consequences for dividend policy.

At present the company has a debt:equity ratio of 1:5, measured in market value terms. It does not want to increase this ratio at the present time but might need to borrow to pay a maintained dividend in the future.

The senior managers of the company are discussing a range of issues concerning financial strategy in general and dividend policy in particular. One option under consideration is to repurchase some of the company's shares in the coming year using the forecast cash surplus, the aim being to reduce the amount of cash needed to pay dividends in subsequent years.

Required

(a) Summarise the benefits and the dangers to a company of share repurchase as an alternative to dividend payments. (10 marks)

(b) Suggest the advantages and disadvantages of borrowing money to pay dividends in years 2 and 3. (6 marks)

(c) What will be the likely effect on the company's cost of equity if the company decides on share repurchase and/or further borrowing? (4 marks)

(20 marks)

TREASURY MANAGEMENT

Questions 14 to 16 cover treasury management, included in Part B of the BPP Study Text for Risk Management.

14 LIME PLC

(a) Explain the term 'risk management' in respect of interest rates and discuss how interest rate risk might be managed by a company that has a large amount of debt capital in its financing structure. (12 marks)

(b) Lime plc invests temporary cash surpluses in short-term deposits. The treasurer of the company has forecast the following cash movements, and associated probabilities, for the next two months. By the end of month 3, the company will have a much lower cash surplus and possibly a cash deficit.

		Probability
Cash available now	£200,000	1.0
Net cash flow in month 1	+ £400,000	0.4
	+ £600,000	0.6
Net cash flow in month 2	- £650,000	0.5
	- £750,000	0.5

Assume that all movements of cash take place on the last day of each month.

The structure of short-term interest rates is currently as follows.

Maturity period	*Interest rate*
1 month	6.5%
2 months	6.6%

Economic forecasters expect interest rates to rise, and in one month's time they are expected to be 6.8% per annum for one-month deposits. Transaction costs are £150 per transaction below £600,000 and £200 per transaction in excess of this amount.

Required

(i) Calculate the estimated cash balances at the end of months 1 and 2.

(ii) Recommend, with reasons, how the cash surpluses available between now and the end of month 2 should be deposited to maximise before-tax income.

(8 marks)

(20 marks)

15 CENTRALISATION AND RISK DATA

(a) An international group based in the UK has a large number of subsidiaries in both the UK and other countries. The parent company has adopted a management philosophy of decentralisation, and 'local managers' of subsidiaries are given the responsibility for most decision-making below group board level. The responsibilities of the subsidiary managers include decisions about borrowing and investing surplus cash (subject to the group board's policy on maximum borrowing levels), hedging financial risk, and agreeing transfer prices for transactions between subsidiaries in the group.

The group finance director, whilst supporting the idea of decentralised management, has suggested that the group could stand to benefit substantially by the creation of a treasury department at head office, and that treasury management within the group should be centralised.

The operations director for the group is concerned about the effect this will have on the management of the subsidiaries.

Required

(i) What does 'centralisation of treasury management' mean?

(ii) What are the potential benefits of centralising the group treasury function?

(iii) What are the potential problems for subsidiaries, and how might they be dealt with? (10 marks)

(b) Your company has purchased the following data which provide scores of the political risk for a number of countries in which the company is considering investing in a new subsidiary.

	Total	*Economic performance*	*Debt in default*	*Credit ratings*	*Political stability*	*Remittance restrictions*	*Access to capital*
Weighting	100	25	10	10	25	15	15
Gmala	37	13	4	5	5	10	0
Forland	52	5	10	9	16	8	4
Amapore	36	12	2	3	9	5	5
Covia	30	9	3	2	15	1	0
Settia	39	15	4	3	11	4	2

Countries have been rated on a scale from 0 up to the maximum weighting for each factor (eg 0-15 for remittance restrictions). A high score for each factor, as well as overall, reflects low political risk.

A proposal has been put before the company's board of directors that investment should take place in Forland.

Required

As financial adviser, prepare a brief report for the company's board of directors discussing whether or not the above data should form the basis for:

(i) The measurement of political risk; and (5 marks)
(ii) The decision about which country to invest in. (5 marks)

(20 marks)

16 TREASURY MANAGEMENT

Many large international organisations have a central treasury department, which might be a separate profit centre within the group. The responsibilities of this department will include the management of business risk and market risk for the group as a whole.

Required

(a) What might be the functions of a central treasury department? (4 marks)

(b) What is the difference between business risk and market risk, and what is the role of the treasury department in relation to business risk and market risk? (6 marks)

(c) What information does the treasury department need, from inside and outside the organisation, to perform its function? (6 marks)

(d) Explain briefly how cash budgeting and control of cash flow can be used to manage short-term financial risk. (4 marks)

(20 marks)

HEDGING CURRENCY RISK

Questions 17 to 25 cover hedging currency risk, included in Part B of the BPP Study Text for Risk Management.

17 EXCHANGE RATES

(a) It is currently December 20X4. Your managing director has received forecasts of exchange rates for the US dollar against sterling in two years' time from three leading banks.

£/$ forecasts of the spot rate at 31 December 20X6

Topbank	1.35
Superbank	1.55
Strongbank	1.68

The current spot rate is £1/ $1.5240.

A non-executive director of your company has suggested that in order to forecast future exchange rates, the interest rate differential between countries should be used as the basis for the forecast. The current two-year interest rates are 5.75% on sterling and 6.50% on the US dollar.

Required

You have been asked by your managing director to prepare a brief report discussing:

(i) The likely validity of the non-executive director's comment, and the relationship between spot and forward exchange rates (5 marks)

(ii) Possible reasons for the wide spread of forecasts by the banks. (5 marks)

(b) A company in the UK has agreed to sell goods to an importer in the US at an invoiced price of $150,000. Of this amount, $60,000 will be payable on shipment, $45,000 one month after shipment and $45,000 three months after shipment.

The quoted £/$ exchange rates at the date of shipment are as follows.

Spot	1.4900 - 1.4920
One month	1.4870 - 1.4900
Three months	1.4800 - 1.4840

The company decides to enter into appropriate forward exchange contracts through its bank to hedge these transactions.

Required

(i) State what are the presumed advantages of doing this.

(ii) Calculate the sterling amount that the company would receive.

(iii) Comment with hindsight on the wisdom of hedging in this instance, assuming that the spot rates at the dates of receipt of the two instalments of $45,000 were as follows:

First instalment	1.4940 - 1.4960
Second instalment	1.5000 - 1.5040

(7 marks)

(iv) Describe how foreign exchange transactions using futures would differ from those assumed in part (i) of this question. (3 marks)

(20 marks)

18 CURRENCY

(a) The financial press recently listed the following information about two currencies, the Australian dollar (A$) and the Saudi Arabian riyal (SR)

Spot rates:	A$/SR 2.0725
	SR/A$ 0.4825
90 day rates:	A$/SR 2.0687
	SR/A$ 0.4834

The Australian prime interest rate on the same day was 5.5%.

Note. Use a 360-day year.

Required

(i) Explain what is implied about the Saudi Arabian 90-day interest rate.

(ii) Calculate and comment on the Saudi Arabian interest rate if the forward exchange rate was SR/A$ 0.4795.

Calculate and comment on the 90-day forward rate on SR/A$ if the Saudi Arabia interest rate was 5%. (8 marks)

(b) It is currently 20X4. Five or six years ago, Rigby plc, a manufacturing company based in the United Kingdom, developed a substantial market for its products in Eastern Europe. The board decided to establish a subsidiary in Hungary. The assets needed for the new subsidiary were mainly buildings. Plant and equipment were provided from the UK. Most of the raw material for production was, and still is, sourced in the UK. Local labour is used, except for senior managers who are seconded from the UK parent for 2 to 3 years.

Required

Assuming the UK company wished to minimise its exposure to exchange risk:

(i) Discuss the options which were available to the parent company management for financing the new subsidiary. Assume that the parent company did not need to raise new long-term capital to finance this new venture.

(ii) Explain how the UK parent could have minimised its exchange losses arising from either operating transactions or a decline in the value of Hungarian forints (HUF). (12 marks)

(20 marks)

19 CURRENCY EXPOSURE

Fade plc, a merchandising company operating mainly in the UK, undertakes export and import transactions with firms in a less well-developed country, Freiland. Many of these transactions are necessarily conducted in the local currency, the Freimark (FM).

Fade plc also has a small subsidiary company in Freiland, concerned wholly with servicing equipment sold in that country.

The value of the Freimark against the pound has fluctuated frequently over the past 12 months between £1/FM 12.50 and £1/FM 27.50. The exchange rate currently stands at 25.00.

The treasurer of Fade plc has prepared the following cash flow forecast of transactions in Freimarks over the next six months.

	Month 1	*Month 2*	*Month 3*	*Month 4*	*Month 5*	*Month 6*
	FM000	FM000	FM000	FM000	FM000	FM000
Receipts into the UK	40,600	50,100	37,000	80,000	65,000	48,500
Payments for goods imported into Freiland	38,200	55,500	44,200	36,800	53,000	49,500
Purchases of fixed assets for Freiland subsidiary	-	-	-	40,000	4,000	-
	38,200	55,500	44,200	76,800	57,000	49,500
Receipts less payments	2,400	(5,400)	(7,200)	3,200	8,000	(1,000)

Required

(a) State and explain the various factors that should be taken into account before the company decides to take any action to reduce its foreign exchange transaction exposure. (6 marks)

(b) Describe three techniques of exposure management that might be available to Fade plc under the circumstances of this question. (10 marks)

(c) Explain the meaning of 'economic exposure' and distinguish it from transaction exposure. (4 marks)

(20 marks)

20 PARTISAN PLC

Partisan plc is a medium-sized importer and exporter of textile and other heavy machinery. It sells its products world-wide and has a policy of hedging all its overseas transactions in excess of a sterling equivalent of £100,000. Typically the company uses money market hedges or forward contracts. Below £100,000, the company bears the exchange risk itself.

The company's profits after interest for the past two years were as follows:

Year to	*30 September 20X8*	*30 September 20X9*
	£ million	£ million
Profit after interest	2.919	2.026

If the company had *not* hedged its currency risks, the profits would have been £2.141 million in 20X8 and £2.373 million in 20X9.

The Chief Executive is concerned about the effect hedging costs have had on the bottom line, especially as a hedging operation for a large contract is currently being arranged. He has asked for a report with a view to considering changing the company's policy on hedging.

The details of the proposed hedge are as follows.

The company is due to pay a Hong Kong supplier HK$2.75 million in three months' time for machinery for which Partisan plc has already found a buyer within the UK for £300,000. Today's exchange rate is £1/ HKD 11.3193. On the advice of the treasurer, the company is proposing to take out a contract to purchase HK$2.75 million in three months' time at the forward rate of HK$11.2589.

Required

As Financial Manager with Partisan plc, write a report to the Chief Executive explaining:

(a) The purpose of hedging and the advantages and disadvantages of the company's current policy. (6 marks)

(b) The financial implications of the hedging contract currently being considered. For the purposes of illustration and comparison, assume the Hong Kong dollar:

Weakens against sterling in three months' time to 11.8800, and

Strengthens against sterling to 10.9900 (4 marks)

(c) The factors the company should consider before changing its policy, in particular taking a decision not to hedge future foreign currency transactions (6 marks)

(d) Alternative methods of managing currency risks which might be available to the company. (4 marks)

(20 marks)

21 WEFT PLC

Weft plc is an importer/exporter of textiles and textile machinery. It is based in the UK but trades extensively with countries throughout Europe, particularly in the eurozone. It has a small subsidiary based in Germany. The company is about to invoice a customer in Germany for 750,000 euros, payable in three months' time. Weft plc's treasurer is considering two methods of hedging the exchange risk. These are:

Method 1

Borrow €750,000 for three months, convert the loan into sterling and repay the loan out of eventual receipts. The interest payable on the loan will be purchased in the forward exchange market.

Method 2

Enter into a 3-month forward exchange contract with the company's bank to sell €750,000.

The spot rate of exchange is €1.6006 to £1.

The 3-month forward rate of exchange is €1.5935 to £1.

Annual interest rates for 3 months' borrowing are: euro 3%, sterling 5%.

Required

(a) (i) Which of the two methods is the most financially advantageous for Weft plc? (6 marks)

(ii) What are the other factors to consider before deciding whether to hedge the risk using the foreign currency markets? (7 marks)

(b) Assume that Weft plc is trading in and with developing countries rather than Europe and has a subsidiary in a country with no developed capital or currency markets. Weft plc is now about to invoice a customer in that country in the local currency. Advise the company's treasurer about ways in which the risk can be managed in these circumstances. (7 marks)

(20 marks)

22 GAUNT LTD

(a) Discuss the usefulness of interest rate swaps and currency swaps to the financial manager of a fast growing business that is just beginning to trade internationally. (10 marks)

(b) Gaunt Ltd is an importer of goods, mainly from Japan. You have received the following memo from the managing director:

'I have been reading the *Financial Times* and note that the current spot rate for yen is 174.820 to the pound. The three-month forward rate is 172.930 and for 12 months it is even lower, 167.510. I also note that twelve-month interest rates in Japan are only 0.10% per annum, whereas in the UK they are much higher, at 4.5% per annum. I have three suggestions:

(i) If we buy yen on the spot market as and when we need them to pay for our imports, rather than taking out forward contracts, as is our present policy, it should surely save us a lot of money?

(ii) An alternative policy, if you think that sterling will depreciate over the next 12 months, is to buy yen on the spot market now and place them on deposit until we need them.

(iii) Would it not be in our interests to borrow yen and pay off our sterling loans? This would save us money on interest payments.'

Required

Explain how you would respond to each of the managing director's suggestions.

(10 marks)

(20 marks)

23 BAILEY SMALL

Bailey Small plc is an importer/exporter of heavy machinery for a variety of industries. It is based in the UK but trades extensively with the USA. The company does not have a separate treasury function and it is part of your duties to assess and manage currency risks. You are concerned about the recent fluctuations in the exchange rate between US$ and sterling and are considering various methods of hedging the exchange risk involved.

Assume it is now the end of March.

The following transactions are expected on 30 June.

Sales receipts	$450,000
Purchases payable	$250,000

Economic data

1 The spot rate of exchange is £/US$1.6540-1.6590.
2 The US$ premium on the three-month forward rate of exchange is 0.82-0.77 cents.
3 Annual interest rates for three months' borrowing are: USA 6 per cent; UK 9 per cent.
4 Annual interest rates for three months' lending are: USA 4 per cent; UK 6.5 per cent.
5 Currency option prices (cents per £, contract size £12,500):

	Calls		*Puts*	
Exercise price, $	*June*	*September*	*June*	*September*
1.60	-	15.20	-	-
1.65	2.65	7.75	-	3.45
1.70	1.70	3.60	-	9.32

Assume that there are three months from now to expiry of the June contracts.

Required

(a) Calculate the net sterling receipts that Bailey Small plc can expect from its transactions if the company hedges the exchange risk using each of the following alternatives:

(i) The forward foreign exchange market
(ii) The money market

Accompany your calculations with brief explanations of your approach and recommend the most financially advantageous alternative for Bailey Small plc. Assume transaction costs would be 0.2 per cent of the US$ transaction value under either method, paid at the beginning of the transaction (i.e. now). (8 marks)

(b) Discuss the relative advantages and disadvantages of using foreign currency options compared with fixed forward contracts. To illustrate your arguments assume that the actual spot rate in three months' time is 1.6458-1.6513, and assess whether Bailey Small plc would have been better advised to hedge using options, rather than a fixed forward contract. (12 marks)

(20 marks)

24 BRIE SA

Brie SA is a French company which trades frequently with the USA.

Transactions to be completed within the next three months are as follows.

	Receipts	*Payments*
3 months time	\$4.8m	\$7.6m

Exchange rates in Paris

	\$/Euro
Spot	1.0610 – 1.0661
3 months forward	1.0656 – 1.0715
6 months forward	1.0683 – 1.0740

Euro market traded option prices (62,500 euro contract size) in the USA
(The options relate to the purchase or sale of euros)

Exercise price (€/\$)	*June contracts*		*September contracts*	
	Calls	*Puts*	*Calls*	*Puts*
0.936	1.65	0.41	2.38	0.71
0.938	0.56	1.20	1.01	1.57
0.940	0.17	2.65	0.48	3.45

Option premiums are in cents per euro and are payable up front. The options are American style.

If the company uses options, it will buy dollars at the spot rate in exchange for euros.

Assume that it is now 15 June and that option contracts mature on the 15th of the month.

Required

(a) Explain the meaning of transaction and translation exposure and discuss their importance to the financial manager. (7 marks)

(b) How would the company hedge its foreign exchange risk during the next six months using a forward exchange contract? (3 marks)

(c) How would the company hedge its foreign exchange risk during the next six months using a using a currency option with a strike rate of €/\$0.938? (6 marks)

(d) Assuming that a currency option is used and the spot rate on 15 September is €/\$0.9700, what action would the company take? (4 marks)

(20 marks)

25 BLUNT PLC

(a) Blunt plc, a UK registered company, operates in four foreign countries, with total foreign subsidiary turnover of the equivalent of £60 million. The managing director is conducting a strategic review of the company's operations, with a view to increasing operations in some markets, and to reducing the scale of operations in others. He has assembled economic and other data on the four countries where subsidiaries are located which he considers to be of particular interest.

A non-executive director believes that the meeting should not be focusing on such long-term strategic or economic dimensions. He has just read the report of the finance director who has forecast a foreign exchange loss on translation of the net assets of the company's foreign subsidiaries. The forecast loss on translation is £15 million for the current financial year.

The non-executive director is concerned with the detrimental impact he expects this loss to have on the company's share price. He further suggests a number of possible hedging strategies to be undertaken by Blunt's foreign subsidiaries in order to reduce the exposure and the consolidated loss. These include:

(i) Early collection of foreign currency receivables
(ii) Early repayment of foreign currency loans
(iii) Reducing stock levels in foreign countries

Required

Give reasoned advice as to the benefit to Blunt plc of the non-executive director's suggested hedging strategies. (10 marks)

(b) Blunt has a number of intra-group transactions with its four foreign subsidiaries in six months time, and several large international trade deals with third parties. These are summarised below. Intra-group transactions are denominated in US dollars. All third party international trade is denominated in the currency shown. It is now 1 June.

Intra-group transactions

			US$000		
			Paying company		
Receiving company	*UK*	*Sub 1*	*Sub 2*	*Sub 3*	*Sub 4*
UK	-	300	450	210	270
1	700	-	420	-	180
2	140	340	-	410	700
3	300	140	230	-	350
4	560	300	110	510	-

Required

Explain and demonstrate how multilateral netting might be of benefit to Blunt plc.

(10 marks)

(20 marks)

HEDGING INTEREST RATE RISK

Questions 26 to 33 cover hedging interest rate risk, included in Part B of the BPP Study Text for Risk Management.

26 PLANKTON PLC

(a) Plankton plc wishes to raise €100 million in floating rate finance for a period of five years. Discuss the advantages and disadvantage of raising such funds through:

(i) Direct borrowing from a domestic banking system such as the German domestic banking system. (Detailed knowledge of the German banking system is not required)

(ii) The eurocurrency market (5 marks)

(b) Plankton could borrow in euros at euribor + 0.75%.

Plankton's bank has suggested a five-year cross-currency swap as an alternative to direct borrowing in euros. Plankton would issue a five-year sterling fixed rate bond at an interest rate of 7%, and make the following swap with a German company that is also a client of the bank.

Plankton would pay the Germany company euribor + 1% per year on notional principal of €100 million. The German company would pay Plankton 7.5% per year on an equivalent notional principal amount in sterling.

The exchange rate for the notional principal amounts will be today's middle spot foreign exchange rate, and there will be an actual exchange of currency amounts at this exchange rate at the end of the swap term in five years' time. The German company can borrow fixed rate in sterling at 8.5% per annum, and floating rate finance in euros at euribor + 1.5%.

Exchange rate

Spot £/€ 1.5790 – 1.5806

Required

(i) Explain what cash flows would arise for Plankton for the bond issue and the swap, assuming that the bond payments and swap payments occur annually, and suggest whether the arrangement could be of financial benefit to the company. (9 marks)

(ii) Excluding cheaper finance, discuss the possible benefits and the possible risks of such a swap for the two companies and the intermediary bank. (6 marks)

(20 marks)

27 EUNOMIA LTD

Eunomia Ltd is engaged in the manufacture of toiletries and cosmetics that have not been either synthetically processed or tested on animals. Recently, it has developed a new type of moisturising cream based on plant extracts and now wishes to launch this product. The company estimates that the additional costs of equipment and working capital necessary to manufacture the new product would be £400,000. The company intends to borrow the funds required and is confident that the funds will only be required for the first nine months of the product's life. At the end of nine months, the sale of a patent relating to another product will be used to repay the amount owed.

The company can finance the new product either by a fixed rate loan or a floating rate loan. As at early June 20X5 ('now'), the fixed rate loan will attract an annual interest rate of 8.5% and the issue costs will be 1.5% of the loan requirement. The floating rate loan will attract an initial annual interest rate of 8% which will be subject to quarterly reviews. The issue costs of the floating rate loan will be 2% of the loan requirement. Interest rates have moved significantly in recent months and future interest rate movements are likely. The following quarterly movements in interest rates and their probability of occurrence have been estimated for the period of the loan.

Interest rate movements

	Change from current rate in quarter commencing early September 20X5		*Change from previous quarter in quarter commencing early December 20X5*	
	Increase	Decrease	Increase	Decrease
Percentage points	2.0	3.0	2.5	2.5
Probability of occurrence	0.8	0.2	0.5	0.5

Ignore taxation and the time value of money.

Required

(a) Calculate the *expected cost* to Eunomia Ltd of both types of loan capital over the period for which the funding is required, and discuss your findings (10 marks)

(b) For a company with floating rate interest on its borrowings, discuss two ways that it could hedge against the risk of an increase in interest rates. (10 marks)

(20 marks)

28 GROUND PLC

(a) Ground plc wishes to raise £15 million of floating rate finance. The company's bankers have suggested using a five-year swap. Ground plc has an AA credit rating and can issue fixed rate finance at 7.35%, or floating rate at LIBOR plus 60 basis points.

Putter plc has a BBB credit rating. It wants to raise fixed rate finance for five years. It can borrow in the bond market at a fixed rate of 8.8%, or in the loans market at a floating rate of LIBOR + 1.35%.

Centre Bank, which specialises in interest rate swaps, is quoting rates for five-year swaps of 7.25% - 7.00%.

Twelve-month LIBOR is currently 7.10%.

Required

(a) Explain the main reasons why a company other than a financial institution might wish to arrange interest rate swaps. (6 marks)

(b) Evaluate whether or not each company would be interested in arranging a swap with Centre Bank, and if so, by how much they would benefit. (10 marks)

(c) Estimate the present value of the differences in cash flow that would exist for Ground plc from using a swap rather than borrowing at a floating rate directly in the market if LIBOR moves to 7.8% after one year and then remains constant.

The market may be assumed to be efficient and assume that the discount rate to apply is 9%.

Swap interest payments and interest payments on the company's actual loan will be paid annually at the end of the year concerned.

Comment upon your findings, and discuss whether they would be likely to influence a decision by Ground plc to undertake a swap. (4 marks)

(20 marks)

Discount rates at 9%

Year	
0	1.00
1	0.92
2	0.84
3	0.77
4	0.71
5	0.65

29 QW PLC

Assume that you are treasurer of QW plc, a company with diversified, international interests. The company wishes to borrow £10 million for a period of three years. Your company's credit rating is good and current market data suggests that you could borrow at a fixed rate of interest at 8 per cent per annum or at a floating rate of LIBOR + 0.20 per cent per annum. You believe that interest rates are likely to fall over the next three years, and favour borrowing at a floating rate.

Your company's bankers are currently working on raising a three-year £10 million loan for another of their customers, ER plc. This company is smaller and less well known than QW plc, and its credit rating is not as high. ER plc could borrow at a fixed rate of 9.5 per cent per annum or a floating rate of LIBOR + 0.90 per cent. ER plc has indicated to the bank that it would prefer a fixed-rate loan.

Your bankers have suggested both companies should engage in a swap which might benefit both companies. The bank would act as the counterparty for each company, so two separate swap agreements would be made. The bank's profit would be 0.20 per cent. It has been agreed that the benefits should be shared equally between QW and ER.

Assume that interest is paid at the end of each twelve-month period of the loan's duration and that the principal is repaid on maturity (i.e. at the end of three years).

Some board members have expressed concern about using financial derivatives and worry that your activities may be involving the company in unnecessary risk.

Required

Write a report to the board which:

(a) Explains the meaning and use of financial derivatives, in general terms, and the advantages and disadvantages of their use for companies such as QW plc (6 marks)

(b) Describes the characteristics and benefits of interest rate swaps compared with other forms of interest rate risk management, such as forward rate agreements and interest rate futures (6 marks)

(c) Explains the course of action necessary to implement the swap being considered with ER plc, and calculates and comments on the financial benefits to be gained from the operation. (8 marks)

(20 marks)

30 ARK PLC

The corporate treasury team of Ark plc are debating what strategy to adopt towards interest rate risk management. The company's financial projections show an expected cash deficit in three months time of £12 million, which will last for a period of three months. Base rate is currently 6% per year, and Ark plc can borrow at 1.5% over base, or invest at 1% below base. The treasury team believes that economic conditions are such that there could be a substantial increase in interest rates soon, of about 2% per year, but this is by no means certain.

In the UK, the economy is still recovering from a recession and representatives of industry are calling for interest rates to be cut by 1%. Even so, the corporate treasury team believes that interest rates are more likely to rise than to fall, and does not want interest payments during the three-month period to increase by more than £10,000 from the amounts that would be paid at current interest rates. It is now 1 December.

LIFFE prices (1 December)

Futures: LIFFE £500,000 three-month sterling interest rate (points of 100%)

December	93.75
March	93.45
June	93.10

Options: LIFFE £500,000 short sterling options (points of 100%)

Exercise price	*Calls March*	*Puts March*
9200	3.33	-
9250	2.93	-
9300	2.55	0.92
9350	2.20	1.25
9400	1.74	1.84
9450	1.32	2.90
9500	0.87	3.46

Required

(a) How much interest will the company have to pay in the three months under review, if the base rate does not change at all over the next three months. Assume for the purpose of interest calculations that three months' interest would be exactly one quarter of a full year's interest. (2 marks)

(b) Illustrate results of futures to hedge the exposure if, by 1 March, the base rate has risen by 2% and the futures price has moved by 1.8%. (7 marks)

(c) Illustrate results of options on interest rate futures to hedge the exposure if, by 1 March, the base rate has risen by 2% and the futures price has moved by 1.8%. Assume that you select options with a strike rate of 93.50. (7 marks)

(d) Describe two other instruments that could be used to hedge the company's interest rate exposure. (4 marks)

(20 marks)

31 SLICE COMMUNICATIONS

The monthly cash budget of Slice Communications plc shows that the company is likely to need £18 million in two months' time for a period of three months. Financial markets have recently been volatile, due to uncertainties about the international political situation. The finance director of Slice fears that short-term interest rates could rise by as much as 150

basis points in the next month or so. If the political situation stabilises, short-term rates could fall by 50 basis points. Three-month LIBOR is currently 6.5% and HYK plc can borrow at LIBOR + 0.75%.

The finance director does not wish to pay more than 7.50%, including option premium costs, but excluding the effect of margin requirements and commissions.

LIFFE £500,000 3 month futures prices. The value of one tick is £12.50

December	93.40
March	93.10
June	92.75

LIFFE £500,000 3 months options prices (premiums in annual %)

Exercise		*Calls*			*Puts*	
price	*December*	*March*	*June*	*December*	*March*	*June*
92.50	0.33	0.88	1.04	-	-	0.08
93.00	0.16	0.52	0.76	-	0.20	0.34
93.50	0.10	0.24	0.42	0.18	0.60	1.93
94.00	-	0.05	0.18	0.36	1.35	1.92

Assume that it is now 1 December and that exchange-traded futures and options contracts expire at the end of the month. Margin requirements and default risk may be ignored.

Required

(a) Estimate the results of undertaking

(i) an interest rate futures hedge on the LIFFE exchange, and

(ii) a hedge using options on futures at a strike rate of 93.50

if LIBOR were to increase by 150 basis points by the time that the company wishes to borrow, but that the futures price shows an increase in the interest rate of just 130 basis points.

Discuss for each hedging method how successful the hedge would have been.

State clearly any assumptions that you make. (10 marks)

(b) Discuss the relative advantages of using exchange-traded interest rate options and over-the-counter (OTC) interest rate options. (6 marks)

(c) Your finance director has received some quotations for over-the-counter (OTC) interest rate options and wonders whether or not they are too expensive. Outline the main determinants of interest rate option prices, and comment upon whether or not the OTC options are likely to be expensive. (4 marks)

(20 marks)

32 FUTURES AND OPTIONS

(a) The board of directors of your company is considering the use of financial futures by the company to hedge its financial exposures. Prepare a brief report for the board of directors outlining the possible advantages of financial futures for a large manufacturing company, what risks there might be in using financial futures as a hedge, and how any risks of using financial futures might be minimised. (10 marks)

(b) The directors of Toast plc are considering the use of options to protect the current interest yield from their company's £9.75 million short-term money market investments. Having made initial enquiries they have been discouraged by the cost of the option premium. A member of the treasury staff has suggested the use of a collar as this would be cheaper. Protection is required for the next eight months.

Assume that it is now 1 June.

LIFFE interest rate options on three-month money market futures

The contract size is £500,000, and the premium cost is in annual %. The tick size is 0.01% and the price per tick is £12.50.

	Calls		*Puts*	
	Dec	*March*	*Dec*	*March*
9100	0.90	1.90	-	0.02
9150	0.56	1.45	0.05	0.06
9200	0.27	1.04	0.17	0.13
9250	0.09	0.68	0.45	0.24
9300	0.01	0.20	0.83	0.32
9350	-	0.05	1.13	0.54

The current interest rate the company receives on its short-term money market investments is 7.5% per annum. Assume that the company can buy or sell options at the above prices. Commission, taxation and margins may be ignored.

Required

Discuss how, and estimate at what cost, a collar can be created with options on futures, to protect against the interest yield risk. Use the market data in the table above to illustrate your answer. (10 marks)

(20 marks)

33 OPTIONS AND SWAPS

(a) Financial projections show that your company is likely to have a cash flow deficit of approximately £5 million for a period of three months commencing 1 May next year. It will be necessary for your company to borrow short-term funds during this period. The company can currently borrow at LIBOR + 1.5%.

Short-term interest rates are believed to be more likely to increase than to decrease although, if there is a fall in the retail prices index during the next few months, interest rates could decrease. Experts at your company's bank believe that LIBOR could increase by up to 1% or decrease by up to 0.75% during the next four months.

LIBOR is currently 7%.

LIFFE three-month Sterling futures, £500,000 contract size, £12.50 tick size

March	92.75
June	92.50

LIFFE option price on three-month Sterling futures. £500,000 contract size, £12.50 tick size

	Premium (%)			
	Calls		*Puts*	
Exercise price	*March*	*June*	*March*	*June*
92.00	0.10	0.19	1.30	1.45
93.00	0.28	0.36	0.44	0.59
94.00	0.94	1.20	0.22	0.37

Required

Using options on interest rate futures, suggest a hedging strategy to manage short-term interest rate risks, and calculate the likely impact of your suggested strategy if interest rates were to move to each of the extremes suggested by the experts at the bank.

Assume that it is now 31 December and that contracts mature at the month end. You may also assume that any change in the interest rate will have a direct effect on the futures price.

State clearly any other assumptions that you make. (10 marks)

(b) Suppose your company wishes to raise £15 million of floating rate finance. Your bank has suggested using a five-year swap. The company has an A+ credit rating and can issue fixed rate finance at 8.35%, or floating rate at LIBOR plus 60 basis points. Another company, Bravo plc has only a BBB credit rating and can raise fixed rate finance at 10.8%, or floating rate at LIBOR + 1.35%.

A five-year interest rate swap on a £15 million loan could be arranged with Gigbank acting as an intermediary for a fee of 0.25% per annum. Your company will only agree to the swap if it can make annual savings of at least 30 basis points. LIBOR is currently 8.5%.

Required

(i) Evaluate whether or not the swap is likely to be agreed. (5 marks)

(ii) What would be the consequences of the swap arrangement if the LIBOR rate went up from 8.5% to 10% for the remaining term of the swap? (5 marks)

(20 marks)

CORPORATE GOVERNANCE

Questions 34 to 40 cover corporate governance, the subject of Part C of the BPP Study Text for Risk Management.

34 GOVERNANCE

(a) Briefly explain what is meant by corporate governance and discuss how the main measures recommended by the Combined Code should contribute towards better corporate governance. (10 marks)

(b) Discuss the importance and limitations of ESOPs (executive share option plans) to the achievement of goal congruence within an organisation. (10 marks)

(20 marks)

35 OECD

In 1998, The Organisation for Economic Co-operation and Development issued non-binding principles of corporate governance for its member countries.

Required

(a) What is the main reason for encouraging better corporate governance? (4 marks)

(b) Who, according to the OECD, are the key participants in a corporate governance system? (3 marks)

(c) Describe each of the five broad areas of OECD corporate governance principles. (10 marks)

(d) In a major international car manufacturing company, the common stock consists of Class A and Class B shares. Each Class B share is entitled to 16 times as many votes as a Class A share, and a single family controls 40% of the total votes through its ownership of Class B shares. Comment briefly on this share structure for a global company from the perspective of the OED principles. (3 marks)

(20 marks)

36 NON-EXECUTIVES

It is a principle of corporate governance that the board of directors should be able to exercise an objective judgement on the company's affairs. However, it is recognised that potential conflicts of interest can arise between the owners of a company and its management. As a means of dealing with the potential conflicts of interest, it was recommended by the Cadbury Committee in the UK that the boards of companies with a London Stock Exchange listing should appoint a minimum number of non-executive directors (NEDs). A distinction was also made between independent and non-independent non-executive directors.

A variety of criticisms have been made of the system of NEDs. These include the argument that many non-executives are executive directors of other major companies, which restricts their willingness to speak out on the company's affairs. NEDs have also been criticised for holding a non-executive post with too many companies, sometimes five or even more.

In the UK, some criticism has also been voiced against the growing practice of paying NEDs partly in shares or share options of the company.

Required

(a) Explain the distinction between independent and non-independent NEDs. (3 marks)

(b) What are the main areas for a potential conflict of interest between the shareholders of a company and the executive directors? Explain how the use of non-executive directors should help to deal with this problem. (7 marks)

(c) What might be the implications for the integrity or the effectiveness of NEDs of appointing executives of other large companies to non-executive positions, and of holding several NED positions at the same time? (6 marks)

(d) In your view, what might be the objections to paying NEDs in shares or share options of the company, and do you agree with those objections? (4 marks)

(20 marks)

37 AUDIT AND GOVERNANCE

(a) What is the role of the external auditors in contributing towards a proper system of corporate governance, and what is the relationship between the auditors and the audit committee? (6 marks)

(b) What are internal controls and what is their purpose in a system of risk management? (6 marks)

(c) What would an internal audit department contribute towards risk management, and what are the Turnbull Committee recommendations on internal audit in listed companies? (6 marks)

(d) A recommendation of the Combined Code is that the positions of chief executive and chairman should not be held by the same person. What is the reason for this recommendation? (2 marks)

(20 marks)

38 REMUNERATION

The remuneration of executive directors is a controversial issue for corporate governance, and there is growing acceptance that remuneration systems should be logically-based and fair. The Combined Code on corporate governance states that: 'Levels of remuneration should be sufficient to attract, retain and motivate executive directors needed to run the company successfully, but companies should avoid paying more than is necessary for this purpose. A proportion of executive directors' remuneration should be structured so as to link rewards to corporate and individual performance.'

However, there is also widespread condemnation of 'fat cat' salaries and rewards, and criticisms of senior executives being force to resign when their company has performed very badly, but taking a large pay-off when they leave. In some cases, non-executive directors on remuneration committees have been accused of failing to do their job properly by allowing excessive remuneration packages.

Required

(a) What bases might be used for measuring the performance of senior executives, with a view to establishing a remuneration system that rewards individuals for achievement? (7 marks)

(b) What are the basic principles that should be applied to test the acceptability of a performance measure? (4 marks)

(c) What guidelines have been issued by the Association of British Insurers (ABI) for share incentive schemes for executives? (6 marks)

(d) Suggest two measures that could be taken either to monitor the remuneration packages awarded by remuneration committees, and or to limit the 'rewards for failure' to executives who are forced to resign but take with them a large pay-off. (3 marks)

(20 marks)

39 GOVERNANCE AND CONTROLS

(a) Corporate governance issues first came to prominence in the late 1980s and early 1990s, and triggered the requirement for companies with shares traded on the main stock market to have a system of corporate governance in place.

Required

What were the main issues that triggered the requirement for systematised corporate governance in large public companies? (6 marks)

(b) A UK public company has an official listing for its shares, which are traded on the London Stock Exchange. The company has a small head office, including a non-executive chairman, a chief executive and a finance director. There are three major business divisions, each headed by a main board member, and each business division consists of a number of operating units (subsidiaries). The management structure is largely decentralised, and many operating and spending decisions are taken at operating unit level. Operations are carried on throughout Europe. The board consists of five executive directors, a non-executive chairman, and five non-executive directors. There is no internal audit department.

The board is required to make an annual statement in its report and accounts about the effectiveness of its internal controls.

Required

Explain what the board should do before it is in a position to make a statement about the effectiveness of its internal controls. Give particular attention to the need for a control environment, the evaluation of risks, the existence of information and communication systems, control procedures and monitoring and corrective action.

(14 marks)

(20 marks)

40 OBJECTIVES AND INCENTIVES

(a) You are an adviser to a large multinational company whose shares are listed in a number of international stock markets. The company is reviewing its corporate plan, and the non-executive directors have expressed concern about a number of issues.

(i) At present, the company focuses on maximising shareholder wealth. All the executive directors are on an incentive scheme whereby they are paid an annual bonus based on the increase in the share price over the past 12 months. They have all received share options under an executive option scheme. In the past five years, bonuses have been paid on three occasions, when the share price rose, and no bonus was paid in the other two years, when the share price fell. The share price now stands just 15% above where it was five years ago.

(ii) Apart from the directors, no other executives benefit from an incentive scheme.

(iii) The company has a poor public image, and has been accused in the press and by environmental pressure groups of damaging the environment and having no sense of social responsibility.

(iv) Three months ago, following poor interim results for the first six months of the year, and the issue of a profit warning by the company, the operations director was dismissed. His 'pay off' was in the region of £1.5 million.

A committee of non-executive directors has met to discuss corporate objectives and the apparent lack of common interest between shareholders, directors, and other executives, and also the company's poor image with the public and possibly with customers.

Required

As financial adviser, write a report to the senior non-executive director of the company about the company corporate objective and the incentive schemes that are in place. In your report, you should explain why shareholder wealth maximisation might be taken as the single objective for the company, and why the multinational company appears to have had only small success in achieving this objective. Suggest ways in which the apparent conflicts of interest between shareholders, directors, managers, customers and the public might be lessened. (14 marks)

(b) The company is already considering improving the methods of remuneration for its senior employees. As a member of the executive board, you are asked to give your opinions on the following suggestions:

(i) A high basic salary with usual 'perks' such as company car, pension scheme etc, but no performance-related bonuses

(ii) A lower basic salary with usual 'perks' plus a bonus related to their division's profit before tax

(iii) A lower basic salary with usual 'perks' plus a share option scheme which allows senior employees to buy a given number of shares in the company at a fixed price at the end of each financial year

Required

Discuss the arguments for and against *each* of the *three* options from the point of view of both the company and its employees. Detailed comments on the taxation implications are *not* required. (6 marks)

(20 marks)

Answers to multiple choice questions

1 B Insurance might be the most appropriate risk hedging strategy when the potential cost is high, but the likelihood of the adverse outcome happening is fairly low. When the frequency is high, internal measures to manage the risk would probably be more appropriate.

2 A

3 D

4 C Risk aversion is not the same as risk avoidance. Risk aversion means not undertaking an investment when an alternative is available offering the same return for less risk, or a higher return for the same risk.

5 C This can be measured statistically, given probability estimates of expected returns.

6 A Aversion to risk means undertaking a project with higher risk only if its expected return is also higher. The company will look for the highest return for the lowest risk, which in this case is Project W.

7 A A risk-averse company will not select a project that offers a lower return for a higher risk. Project W has higher risk than Project X, but offers a lower return. The other three investments all offer either a higher return or a lower risk compared with any of the other projects, and a risk-averse company might choose any of the three.

8 A Ratings Ba and B are speculative grade ratings, not investment grade. Rating BBB is in the Standard & Poor's rating system, not Moody's.

9 D Applying the purchasing power parity principle:

$$\text{Future rate} = \text{Spot rate} \times \frac{\text{Annual inflation rate in Singapore}}{\text{Annual inflation rate in the UK}}$$

$$= 2.45 \times (1.02 \text{ per annum}/1.05 \text{ per annum})$$

$$= 2.38 \text{ approx.}$$

The Singapore dollar will therefore appreciate/sterling will depreciate by (2.45 – 2.38)/2.45 = 2.9% per annum, say 3% per annum, or 6% over the two-year period.

10 D Financial gearing – ie the proportion of debt in the company's capital structure – does not affect operating profits, which are measured before deducting interest. Operating profit volatility is affected, however, by 'operational gearing', which is concerned with the ratio of contribution to sales turnover.

11 D

	£m
Initial earnings (14p × 50 million shares)	7.0
Tax (× 3/7)	3.0
Profit before tax	10.0
Interest (8% of £100 million)	8.0
Operating profit (= profit before interest and tax)	18.0
Increase by 10%	1.8
	19.8
Less interest	8.0
Profit before tax	11.8

Profit before tax would rise from £10 million to £11.8 million, by 18%, and profit after tax and EPS would increase by the same proportion.

12 A Structural hedging is a form of hedging currency risks through matching. Matching involves setting receipts in one currency against expenditures in the same currency: if these match exactly, currency risk is eliminated. Structural hedging is concerned with matching assets and liabilities in any currency. For example, if a manufacturing company has large amounts of income in US dollars, it should site its production facilities in the US or a country whose currency is tied to the US dollar.

13 C

14 B The sensitivity measurement is the percentage change in the value of the item that would be necessary to reduce the project's NPV to 0.

Variable		*Sensitivity*
Equipment cost	13,700/100,000	13.7%
Revenues	PV of revenues = 3.79 × £50,000 = £189,500. 13,700/189,500	7.2%
Running costs	PV of running costs = 3.79 × £20,000 = £75,800 13,700/75,800	18.1%
Project duration	Annual cash flow £30,000 PV of annual cash flows need to be £100,000 for an NPV of 0. PV of annual cash flows are: Years 1 – 5 (× 3.79) = £113,700 Years 1 – 4 (× 3.17) = £95,100 Approx discounted breakeven $= 4 \text{ years} + \frac{100{,}000 - 95{,}100}{113{,}700 - 95{,}100}$ = 4.3 years. (5.0 – 4.3)/5 years	14.0%

15 A The sensitivity measurement is the percentage change in the value of the item that would be necessary to reduce the project' NPV to 0.

PV of revenues = £200,000 × 3.61 = £722,000
PV of running costs = 3.61 × £120,000 = £433,200
NPV = £(722,000 – 433,200 – 200,000) = £88,800

Variable		*Sensitivity*
Equipment cost	88,800/200,000	44.4%
Revenues	88,800/722,000	12.3%
Running costs	88,800/433,200	20.5%
Project duration	Annual cash flow £80,000 PV of annual cash flows need to be £200,000 for an NPV of 0. PV of annual cash flows are: Years 1 – 5 (× 3.61) = £288,800 Years 1 – 4 (× 3.04) = £243,200 Years 1 – 3 (× 2.40) = £192,000 Approx discounted breakeven $= 3 \text{ years} + \frac{200{,}000 - 192{,}000}{243{,}200 - 192{,}000}$ = 3.15 years. (5.0 – 3.15)/5 years	37.0%

16 B Expected return = 3.5% + 0.85 (6 – 3.5)% = 5.625%

17 C Return = 4% + 1.2 (6 – 4)% + 2% = 8.4%

18 A Return = 3% + 0.8 (- 5 – 3)% = - 3.4%

19 C Unsystematic risk is particular to a particular company's shares, and can be hedged through diversifying into a portfolio of investments.

20 B A zero beta indicates a risk-free investment.

Return = 3% + 0 (6%) = 3%.

21 D Given identical companies except for gearing, the beta factor of equity shares will increase with the gearing level. The beta of Y is therefore above the beta for X but below the beta for Z. The beta of W, which is the least-geared of the four companies, is therefore the lowest of the four companies. It must therefore be less than 0.90.

22 B Cost of equity = 5% + 1.10 (9 – 5)% = 9.4%

	Market value	*Cost*	*Weighting*
	£m		£m
Equity	80	0.0940	7.52
Debt	47	0.0525	2.47
	127		9.99

WACC = (9.99/127) × 100% = 7.87%

23 B Dividend cover is the ratio of distributable profits for the year divided by the dividends for the year. When the ratio is less than 1, dividends have exceeded profits for the year. Some of the dividend must therefore have been paid out of retained profits from previous years.

24 C Smoothing annual dividend payments, trying to maintain a steady long-term dividend pay-out ratio and using dividends as a signal to the markets are all aspects of dividend policy. However, residual dividend theory is that companies should use all their profits to reinvest in projects with a positive NPV, and pay out in dividend only the profits left over after these investments have been made.

25 D This is consistent with the Modigliani-Miller theory of the irrelevance of dividend policy to shareholder value.

Equity value

Policy 1: Current year dividend £3 million. Dividend growth = 10% of the 25% of profits retained = 2.5% per annum.

$$\text{Value} = £3 \text{ million} + \frac{(£3 \text{ million} \times 1.025)}{(0.10 - 0.025)}$$

= £44 million

Policy 2: Current year dividend £2 million. Dividend growth = 10% of the 50% of profits retained = 5% per annum.

$$\text{Value} = £2 \text{ million} + \frac{(£2 \text{ million} \times 1.05)}{(0.10 - 0.05)}$$

= £44 million

Policy 3: Current year dividend £1 million. Dividend growth = 10% of the 75% of profits retained = 7.5% per annum.

$$\text{Value} = £1 \text{ million} + \frac{(£1 \text{ million} \times 1.075)}{(0.10 - 0.075)}$$
$$= £44 \text{ million}$$

26 D Cost of equity in the geared company

= 12% + (1 – 0.20) [(12 – 5) × (50/50)]
= 12% + 5.6% = 17.6%

27 A Profits of A plc double those of B plc.

Value of ungeared company similar in size to B plc = 50% of £100 million = £50 million.

Value of geared company = £50 million + (£20 million × 0.30) = £56 million.

This valuation includes the value of the debt capital which is £20 million.

Value of equity in the geared company = £56 million – £20 million = £36 million.

28 B The put option will be exercised, giving a profit of (250 – 220)p = 30p, but after deducting the cost of the premium, the net gain for the investor is 20p.

29 D When quoting exchange rates, the base currency is stated first and the variable currency second. The quoted rates (C$/SFr) are therefore the quantities of Swiss francs per Canadian dollar. The company is selling Swiss francs, and the bank will buy them at the most favourable rate to itself, which is the higher rate.

SFr 1,000,000/1.0195 = C$980,872.98.

30 C Place on deposit $143,000.

Interest for three months = $143,000 × 5% × 3/12 = $1,787.5

Sell forward ($143,000 + 1,787.5) at $1.4, to earn £103,419.64 after three months. This gives a return of about 3.4% for the period on the original £100,000.

31 D Japanese forward rates are lower than the spot rates, because they are quoted forward at a premium against sterling. The yen is therefore 'stronger' forward than spot, due to the fact that interest rates are lower in Japan.

The approximate interest rate difference can be calculated as:

(165/17205) × (12/3) × 100% = 3.8%.

The three-month differential has to be converted to an annual interest rate using the factor × (12/3).

32 A Dollars are quoted forward at a premium, which means that the forward bid and ask rates are 1.4734 – 1.4825.

The bank is selling dollars, and will want the more favourable rate, which is 1.4734. (At this rate, it will receive more in sterling for the dollars it sells than at the higher rate of 1.4825).

33 D To hedge an exposure to a fall in short-term interest rates with futures, it is necessary to buy futures. September futures are more appropriate than June futures, since the September futures relate to a three-month interest period from September, whereas the June futures would relate to a three-month interest period starting next June.

34 C The worst possible scenario for a writer of a put is that the price of the option will fall to zero. The loss would then be the difference between the exercise price and zero, ie the exercise price. However, this loss would be offset by the premium received.

35 A Forward discounts are added to the spot rate, which means that the forward rates are 8.7670 – 8.7700. The bank will be buying rands in exchange for dollars, and will apply the rate more favourable to itself, which is the rate that will cost it the lower amount of dollars. This is the 'ask' or 'offer' rate of 8.7700.

Your company will receive R5,000,000/8.7700 = $570,125.43.

36 C Buying put options would probably be the most suitable trade, because the maximum profit from selling call options would be the premium received. However, given the wording of the question, the answer is to buy put options and sell calls.

37 C Greater price volatility increases the likelihood that options will be exercised, and option premiums will therefore rise for both call and put options.

38 B When a futures position makes a loss on the day, extra variation margin will be demanded, to cover the loss on the position. When a position makes a profit, variation margin is paid back.

39 D The US company will want to sell €5 million in two months, and could use futures or options on currency futures to hedge against the risk of a fall in the value of the euro against the dollar between now and then. It can do this by selling euro futures, which are contracts for the sale of euros in exchange for dollars, or it can buy put options on euro futures. (Each future is for €125,000, which means that 40 contracts or options would be needed to hedge the position.)

40 B The combined cost of the two premiums is 75 + 55 = 130.

He has bought a call at 5000 and will exercise it if the index rises above 5,000. However, he will only make a profit overall, allowing for the cost of the options, if the index rises above 5,000 + 130 = 5130.

Similarly, he will exercise the put if the index is below 5,000 at expiry, but to make an overall profit, the index must be more than 130 below 5,000, ie below 4,870.

41 C The option is in-the-money, because an investor could exercise the call to buy a future at 93.50 and sell the future at 94.00, a gain of 0.50. The intrinsic value of an option is the amount by which it is in-the-money. The intrinsic value is therefore 0.50, and the rest of the premium must be its time value.

42 A The put option is out-of-the-money; therefore all the premium represents time value. The option has no intrinsic value.

43 B The profit per contract is (95.79 – 94.91) = 0.88 or 88 ticks.

The value of a tick price movement is 0.0001 × £500,000 × 3/12 = £12.50

Profit per contract = 88 ticks × £12.50 = £1,100.

Profit for three contracts = £3,300.

44 C Maximum profit if the price of the underlying falls to zero =

(100 – 0) minus the premium paid = 100 – 12 = 88

45 C

46 A To hedge an exposure to an increase in the interest rate, a company will buy an FRA. The start of the interest rate period is after 5 months, and the end is after 11 months, so the FRA is 5 v 11.

47 A The reference rate at fixing is 7.25%, which is higher than the FRA rate. The seller (the bank) therefore pays the buyer (the company). The amount of the payment is:

$$\$10m \times (0.0725 - 0.068 \times \frac{92}{360} \times \frac{1}{\left[1 + \frac{(0.0725 \times 92)}{360}\right]} = \$11,290.86$$

48 D The company will buy a 4 v 7 FRA. The bank is undertaking to receive the fixed rate and pay the benchmark LIBOR rate at settlement. The appropriate FRA rate is therefore the higher of the two, ie the bid rate of 5.73%. Since the company can borrow at 1.25% above LIBOR, its effective borrowing rate is fixed at 5.73% + 1.25% = 6.98%.

49 D In the swap, the bank will receive the fixed rate and pay the floating rate. The higher fixed rate will therefore apply, 5.25%.

The company will receive LIBOR in the swap, and pay 5.25% fixed. It will also pay LIBOR + 0.75% on its loan. Its effective net payment is therefore 5.25% + 0.75% = 6.0%

50 A In the swap, the bank would pay the fixed rate and receive the floating (LIBOR). It will therefore quote the lower of the two rates, the bid rate of 6.70%. The company would pay LIBOR in the swap and receive 6.70% fixed. It would also pay 7.4% by issuing bonds. This gives a net effective cost of LIBOR + (7.4 – 6.7)% = LIBOR + 0.70%. If it borrowed at a floating rate, it would pay LIBOR plus 1%. Issuing bonds and arranging a swap would therefore save 0.30% or 30 basis points.

51 A The company wants to pay fixed interest in euros, and will receive sterling interest at LIBOR in return. It will still have net interest costs of 100 basis points, ie 1% on £6 million, in sterling, but all its other interest payments will be in euros. At maturity, the company must pay 10 million euros in exchange for £6 million, ie the final settlement of principal is in the same direction as the interest payments.

52 B Moving payment obligations from one currency to another can be achieved using a cross-currency swap. The main purpose of interest rate swaps for non-financial companies is probably to manage the balance between fixed and floating rate debt. Occasionally, a credit arbitrage opportunity might exist to lower borrowing costs by arranging a swap.

53 A A collar in effect is a series of matching call and put options. The company buys a series of call options, each with a strike rate of 7%, which fixes its maximum net borrowing cost at 7.50% (since the company borrows at LIBOR plus 0.50%). For each call option, the company sells a put option, which reduces the net premium payable. The put options set a floor of 6% to LIBOR, so that the net borrowing cost for the company will not fall below 6.50%.

54 D Compensation payments are made by the bank to the cap holder when the LIBOR rate is higher than the strike rate of 7%. This occurs in period 2, and not in period 1.

The compensation is paid at the end of the interest period, and so the amount payable is not discounted (unlike an FRA).

Payment = £10 million × (7.50% – 7%) × (184/365) = £25,205.48.

55 D The forint is quoted forward at a higher amount, which means that it is weaker forward than spot, and so is quoted forward at a discount to the euro.

Don't forget to annualise the three-month differential.

$$\frac{(263.83 - 259.25)}{259.25} \times \frac{12}{3} = 7.1\%$$

56 C As the exercise price goes up, the value of a call option will fall. For example, the intrinsic value of an in-the-money option would be less. As the value of the three other factors increases, the value of a call option will rise.

57 C To minimise the risk of a fall in the value of the investment due to an increase in market interest rates, the treasurer should select gilts whose value is least affected by interest payments. Short-dated gilts are less sensitive to interest rate changes, because a larger proportion of their value lies in the redemption value rather than the future interest payments. Low coupon gilts are less sensitive to interest rate changes than high coupon gilts, for the same reason. Less of their value arises from future interest payments and more comes from the future redemption value of the bonds. The redemption value is unaffected by interest rate changes.

58 D

59 A

60 D The ABI has expressed its concern about the use of Total Shareholder Return as a measure of performance for incentive schemes (Answer A). Share options, the ABI recommends, should be issued frequently and in small quantities (Answer B). The recommendation about limiting the approval of non-rights issues is that the limit should be 7.5% of the equity within any three-year rolling period (Answer C).

61 C The Turnbull report suggests that listed companies without an internal audit department should regularly review the need for one. It also recommends that the system of controls should be reviewed at least once a year.

62 A The right of shareholders to elect board members and the principle that anti-takeover devices should not be used to protect management from accountability are specified in the OECD guidelines with in the category 'rights of shareholders'. The right of a stakeholder to have legal redress for violation of a legal right is categorised as a principle relating to the role of stakeholders.

63 B The OECD principles do not refer specifically to non-executive directors. A poison pill (an anti-takeover device), calling general meetings at short notice and failing to use an independent auditor are all breaches of the OECD guidelines.

64 B The committee makes nominations for board appointments, but cannot take the decisions on appointments.

65 B The Combined Code does not specify the minimum number of formal board meetings each year, nor an attendance rate for NEDs. It also specifies that a senior NED should

be nominated, even when the roles of chairman and CEO are held by different individuals.

66 B The Greenbury report was the first of the UK reports on corporate governance to recommend the annual publication of a remuneration report.

Answers to practice questions

1 STRUCTURED APPROACH

(a) An approach to risk management should begin with a process of risk identification. Within any organisation, different methods of identifying risks can be taken. Broadly speaking, the approach taken can be top-down, bottom-up, or a combination of the two. With a top-down approach, risks are identified at senior management level. Senior managers might consult with their staff, but the process is driven by them. With a bottom-up approach, the task of identifying risks starts at a fairly junior level in the organisation hierarchy, and gradually works its way up to a senior management level. A bottom-up approach is likely to succeed in identifying many risks at an operational level. A top-down approach is likely to be more successful in judging strategic risks. Input should also be obtained from functional experts, for identifying risks within a particular area. For example, finance staff might be asked to identify what they consider to be the main financial risks facing the organisation.

Risks can be categorised. There are no standard categories of risk, but an organisation might use categories such as operational risk, competitor risk, financial risk, political risk, economic risk, technology risk and security risks.

In the case of an international airline company, major operational risks that might be identified are:

(a) the risk of an airline crash

(b) the risk of damage to other operational assets, such as buildings, due to fire, flooding or theft, and so on

(c) the risk of a crash in a major computer system

(d) the risk of a strike by pilots or cabin crews

(e) the risk of overcrowding at airports used extensively by the airline

(f) the risk of losing a key member of the management team.

Competitor risk would arise from the threat of action by competitors to undermine the market position of the company. The low price service offered by low-cost airlines, for example, might be seen as a threat by the 'major carriers'.

Political risks would arise from the threat of actions or decisions by a government that could have a harmful effect on the company. For example, a government might have the power to make decisions on which airlines should be allowed landing slots at the country's major international airport(s). International airlines are also vulnerable to worldwide political instability, and in particular the threat of wars.

The success of airlines varies with the state of the economy, and airlines are at risk to changes in economic conditions. In an economic downturn, fewer people fly.

Technology risk is the threat from new technology. In the case of airlines, these risks might be low. In recent years, however, a major risk for banks has been the threat posed to traditional banking systems by internet technology, and the possibility of new 'high technology' entrants to the banking market. Banks that do not invest in new technology might lose most of their customers.

Threats to physical security can be a major problem for many organisations. The threat is particularly severe for airlines, which have been affected on numerous occasions by terrorist activities. Security concerns are therefore a key risk issue for all international airlines.

(b) A distinction is made between financial and non-financial risks. Operational risks and security risks are non-financial, although there will be a financial consequence of anything going wrong. Financial risks are risks that arise from changes in financial conditions or circumstances, which have an effect on cash flows, profits and returns.

Categories of financial risk include credit risk, gearing risk, interest rate risk and currency risk. Credit risk is the risk of losses through non-payment of debts by customers. These risks should not be particularly severe for airlines, which are paid in advance for tickets. Gearing risk is the risk arising from heavy borrowing: when operating profits fall, heavily-indebted companies might find it difficult to meet the interest payment obligations on their debts. This is a severe problem for many international airline companies, which are highly-geared.

Interest rate risk is the risk to cash flows of changes in interest rates. Heavily-indebted companies will be exposed to higher interest rates when they have large amounts of floating rate loans, and their competitive position could be affected by falling interest rates when a large proportion of their debts are at a fixed rate. Currency risk is the risk to cash flows from movements in key currency exchange rates. Non-US airlines, which might pay for new aircraft and fuel in US dollars, could be exposed to changes in the value of the dollar.

Having identified the risks facing the organisation, the next stage in a structured approach to risk management should be to carry out some form of risk assessment. Techniques such as risk mapping can be used. Each risk should be assessed from two perspectives: its frequency or probability of occurring, and the severity of its impact when it does occur. The most serious risks are those with a high probability of occurrence, that have a severe impact when they do occur.

Risk quantification involves trying to put a financial value to the risk. The financial value of a risk would be derived from an estimate of the financial effect it might have, were it to occur, and the probability of it happening. This process will involve a large degree of judgement.

(c) Materiality is relevant in risk assessment. Risks that are not material, because they have a low probability of happening, and would have a small impact if they did occur, might be 'ignored' for the purpose of risk management. The focus should be on risks with a high probability of happening, or with a severe financial or operational effect if they did occur, or both, should be the focus of management attention.

Some risks can be insured. These are risks which should be relatively unlikely to happen, but with a severe impact when they do. The risk of a plane crashing is an example. Key man insurance is another example of hedging a particular risk through an insurance policy. With insurance, a company pays the insurer a premium to take over the risk.

A policy for risk management should be decided for other risks. For example, in the case of financial risk, an airline company might decide on a policy for hedging currency risks and interest rate risks, and for setting a maximum level for gearing.

2 PROJECT RISK

(a) The **project-specific risk** for an individual investment project occurs because the cash flows from the project might be higher or lower than expected, for reasons that are specific to the project. The cash flows might have been estimated incorrectly, such as an under-estimate of operating costs or an over-estimate of market demand. (However, if a company invests in a wide range of similar projects, it can be argued that much of this project risk will be diversified away in the normal course of business.) Other risk factors specific to a project could be the location of the project, or the quality of personnel, or the reliability of the equipment to be used.

Competitive risk is the possibility of unexpected effects on the project cash flows (positive or negative), due to the actions of competitors. The actual actions of competitors might differ from the assumptions made by the company when it takes its project investment decision. Companies cannot diversify away competitive risk, but shareholders can, by investing in the shares of the competitor companies.

Industry-specific risk is the risk of unexpected changes to a project's cash flows (positive or negative) from events or changing circumstances in the industry in which the investment is made. Unexpected changes can arise, for example, due to new technology, or a change in the law, or a rise or fall in the price of a key commodity.

International risk is the uncertainty for a project's cash flows caused by exchange rate changes (currency risk) and by political risk in foreign markets. A European company investing in an emerging economy, for example, will be exposed to international risk due to the probable weakness of the currency of the emerging market country, and by the risk of political change in the country (eg a change of government, or a decision to nationalise the industry).

Market risk refers to changes that could occur in market conditions, that will affect the cash flows from the project. These could be unexpected changes in interest rates, or in the rate of inflation, or in the state of the economy.

Each of these risks is a two-way risk, in the sense that the actual cash flows could be either better or worse than expected. For example sales demand could be higher than forecast, a competitor might over-price a rival product, a new law might be introduced that has the effect of boosting demand for the output produced by the project, and exchange rates or interest rates might move favourably.

(b) (i) The return from an investment is the expected cash return. In the case of an investment in shares, returns are measured by dividends and the capital gain (or loss) over time arising from changes in the share price.

Risk is a measure of the possible variations in the expected returns from an investment. The greater the potential variation in cash flows, the greater the risk. One way of measuring risk is to look at the range of possible outcomes from an investment, with returns ranging from the worst possible to the best possible. A more useful approach to risk measurement would be to assess the probability of different possible outcomes, so that the investor has an understanding of the likelihood of what might occur. Where possible outcomes can be measured statistically by probability analysis, risk can be given a statistical value. For share investments, for example, risk is measured as the standard deviation of possible variations in the expected return.

An investor should make a decision whether or not to undertake an investment, or should choose between investments, on the basis of both their expected return and the investment risk. An individual investment decision will depend on the risk attitude of the decision-maker. A 'risk-averse' attitude to risk and return can be contrasted with a 'risk-seeking' attitude.

(ii) A risk-averse investor will not invest in a project with a higher risk unless the higher risk is compensated for by a higher return. For example, suppose that Project A has an expected return of 10%, and the risk has been measured statistically (as a standard deviation of the expected return) at 8%. If an alternative investment, project B, offers a higher return of 12%, but for a higher

risk of 9%, a risk-averse investor might be indifferent between the two. His choice will depend on his risk-return preferences. However, if there is a third project, project C, which offers a return of 10% and risk of 9%, a risk-averse investor would not want to undertake it. This is because the same return is available for less risk, from Project A, and a higher return is available for the same risk, from Project B.

A risk-seeking investor is someone who is willing to invest in a higher-risk project, in the hope of earning higher returns. For example, suppose that project D has a 50% chance of earning a return of 8% and a 50% chance of a return of 12%. The expected return would be 10%. Now suppose that project E has a 50% chance of making a return of 30% and a 50% chance of making a negative return of 10%. The expected return is still 10%, but the risk is much greater than with project D. Depending on his individual risk preferences, a risk-seeking investor might prefer to invest in project E, in the hope of making a 30% return, whereas a risk-averse investor would prefer project D.

3 MEASURING RISK

(a) Financial risk is narrowly defined as the possibility of changes in returns or cash flows arising from unexpected changes in financial factors. The main categories of financial risk are credit risk, gearing risk, interest rate risk and currency risk. Non-financial risk is then defined as the possibility of changes in returns or cash flows arising from unexpected changes in non-financial factors, such as 'business' or 'operational' factors. Non-financial factors arising from business risk would include the possibility of higher or lower revenue than expected, or higher or lower costs, and variations in returns due to unanticipated actions by competitors.

Financial risk can be defined more broadly to mean the possibility that returns will be higher or lower than expected, due to any factor whose impact can be measured in financial terms.

(b) There are different ways of measuring and assessing risk in a project. The simplest approach is to take a view of what is the most likely result or outcome, and what are the worst possible and the best possible outcomes. An investment decision can be taken on the basis of the most likely outcome, but with an appreciation of how much worse or better the result could be. This approach does not have any mathematical aspect at all.

An alternative approach is to assess the probability of different outcomes, and to use these probabilities to calculate the expected value of the project return. An expected value is the average value of all the different outcomes, weighted to reflect their probability of occurrence. If the number of probabilities is fairly small, risk can be assessed in terms of the probability of different outcomes, for example the overall probability that the project will have a negative NPV.

If the number of probabilities is large, the risk can be measured statistically as a standard deviation of the expected return.

An alternative approach to analysing uncertainty is sensitivity analysis. Perhaps the most common form of sensitivity analysis is to ask 'what if' questions, such as what if costs are 5% higher than estimated, what if revenues are 10% lower, what if the project lasts two years less than expected or what will happen if the cash benefits are deferred by 12 months, and so on. Alternatively, the approach to sensitivity analysis might be to measure by how much each estimate would have to be changed for the worse before the project only just broke even.

(c) *Workings*

Year 1

Sales	*Probability*	*Expected value*
units		units
50,000	0.8	40,000
70,000	0.2	14,000
		54,000

Year 1

		£
Expected contribution	54,000 × £6	324,000
Fixed costs		150,000
		174,000

Year 2	*Units sold in year 2*	*Contribution*	*Probability*
Units sold in year 1		£	
50,000	20,000	120,000	(0.8 × 0.4) = 0.32
50,000	40,000	240,000	(0.8 × 0.6) = 0.48
Units sold in year 1			
70,000	50,000	300,000	(0.2 × 0.3) = 0.06
70,000	60,000	360,000	(0.2 × 0.7) = 0.14

Year 2 sales	*Contribution*	*Probability*	*EV of cont'n*
units	£		£
20,000	120,000	0.32	38,400
40,000	240,000	0.48	115,200
50,000	300,000	0.06	18,000
60,000	360,000	0.14	50,400
			222,000
		Fixed costs	150,000
		EV of profit	72,000

Year	*Item*	*Amount*	*Discount factor at 10%*	*EV of NPV*
		£		£
0	Capital outlay	200,000	1.00	(200,000)
1	Cash profit	174,000	0.91	158,340
2	Cash profit	72,000	0.83	59,760
	EV of NPV			18,100

(i) The expected net present value of the project is + £18,100.

(ii) The capital cost would need to increase by more than (18,100/200,000) 9.05% before the EV of the project NPV became negative.

(iii) The EV of sales units in Year 2 is (0.32 × 20,000) + (0.48 × 40,000) + (0.06 × 50,000) + (0.14 × 60,000) = 37,000.

EV of sales	*Units*	*EV of cont'n*	*Discount factor at 10%*	*PV of EV of cont'n*
		£		£
Year 1	54,000	324,000	0.91	294,840
Year 2	37,000	222,000	0.83	184,260
				479,100

Sales volume (and contribution) would need to fall by over (£18,100/£479,100) = 3.8% before the EV of the project NPV became negative.

(iv) An alternative approach to risk assessment would be to calculate the probability of a negative NPV. For example, there is a 0.32 probability that sales will be

50,000 units in Year 1 (profit £150,000) and just 20,000 units in year 2 (loss £50,000). Given a capital outlay of £200,000 the NPV would be negative if this occurred. If sales are 50,000 units in Year 1 (profit £150,000) and 40,000 units in Year 2 (profit £90,000), the EV of the NPV would be (£150,000 × 0.91) + (90,000 × 0.83) - £200,000 = £1,200, and the project would just about have a positive NPV. The overall probability of a negative NPV, on the basis of the probability estimates, is therefore 0.32 or 32%.

4 TREASURER

To: The non-executive directors
From: Deputy treasurer
Date:

Subject: Aspects of financial risk and its management

The purpose of this report is to explain several aspects of financial risk and its relevance to risk management in a company such as ours.

(a) **The meaning of financial risk**

Financial risk can be defined as the possibility of fluctuations in profit, cash flow or the value of assets or liabilities arising from changes in a financial situation or condition. For trading companies, financial risk usually relates to:

(i) the variation in cash flow or profit that would occur if there were to be a change in an exchange rate or an interest rate, or if a creditor were to become a bad debt

(ii) the change in the value of an asset or liability that would arise from a change in an exchange rate or interest rate

(iii) the risk that the company might have insufficient cash when required to meet its payment obligations.

Financial risk is divided into different categories, such as currency risk, interest rate risk, credit risk, and so on.

The word 'risk' has connotations of something going wrong. This is known as 'downside risk'. However, with many aspects of financial risk, the 'risk' is two-way. A change in an interest rate or an exchange rate can have a beneficial effect on cash flows, profits and asset values, rather than an adverse effect. From a management perspective, however, the main concern is to limit the potential impact of downside risk. Measures to limit or even eliminate financial risk is known as 'hedging' the exposure to risk.

(b) **Currency risk**

Currency risk arises from the possibility of variations in cash flows, profits or asset values from a change in an exchange rate. The risk arises when a company makes transactions in a foreign currency and needs to convert foreign currency into a domestic currency or vice versa to complete the transaction. A change in the exchange rate can affect the amount of 'domestic' currency received or paid. Currency risk also arises when a company has an asset denominated in a foreign currency, and intends at some stage to sell the asset. A change in the exchange rate will affect the amount of domestic currency eventually realised from the sale of the asset.

Currency risk can be categorised into translation, transaction and economic exposures. Translation exposures arise from financial reporting, and are not explained here.

(i) A transaction exposure occurs when a company makes a transaction, such as buying goods from abroad or selling goods to a foreign buyer, and the transaction will be settled at a future date in a foreign currency. If a UK company sells goods to a French buyer, for payment in euros in three months' time, there will be an exposure to a fall in the value of the euro against sterling in the three months to settlement. If the euro falls in value, the UK company will obtain less when the money is eventually received and converted into sterling. Similarly, if a UK company buys goods from a US supplier and agrees to pay after two months, it will be exposed to an increase in the value of the dollar against sterling in that two-month period.

Transaction exposures are incurred by either the buyer or the seller (and sometimes both) in international trade, unless the countries of the buyer and seller are in the same currency zone (such as the euro zone).

(ii) An economic exposure is essentially the same as a transaction exposure, except that it relates to business transactions that have not yet been made. It relates to future business transactions. A company in country A selling to customers in country B is exposed to the risk of a rise in the value of its domestic currency against other currencies, which would make it less price-competitive. Similarly, a company that buys materials in a foreign currency has an economic exposure to a fall in the value of its domestic currency against the currency in which it pays for its materials. When economic exposures are significant, a company might need to consider re-locating its operations to a different currency area.

(c) **Interest rate risk**

Interest rate risk arises from the possibility of variations in cash flows, profits or asset values from a change in an interest rate. Changes in interest rates have an impact on any company that owns interest-bearing assets (such as investments in bonds) or has liabilities on which it pays interest (such as bank loans and bonds).

(i) If a company has debts on which it pays floating rate interest, it will pay more or less interest whenever the interest rate changes.

(ii) If a company has fixed-rate debts, it will benefit or lose, compared to rival companies with floating rate debts, whenever market interest rates rise or fall.

(d) **The term structure of interest rates and its relevance to risk management**

The term structure of interest rates is more commonly referred to as the yield curve. It can be thought of as a graph, with interest rate on the y axis and the term to maturity of a financial instrument (such as a loan or a bond) on the x axis. A yield curve shows the interest rate on a particular type of financial instrument for different maturities. When the yield curve is rising, the interest rate is higher on longer-dated instruments or loans than on shorter-dated instruments/loans. When the yield curve is inverse, longer-dated interest rates are lower than shorter-dated rates. Yield curves are produced, typically, for risk-free government bonds, or low-risk money market rates (eg sterling LIBOR), or interest rate swap rates.

The yield curve is relevant to risk management for companies such as ours for two main reasons.

(i) Current interest rates can be used by banks to fix an interest rate for future borrowing or lending. For example, since today's 12 month and 18 month interest rates on sterling are known, a bank is able to fix a rate now, without risk to itself, for a customer to arrange a six-month loan starting in 12 months' time. Forward transactions in short-term interest rates are known as FRAs.

(ii) Similarly, the yield curve in risk-free bonds can be used by banks to offer other instruments for hedging interest rate risk, such as swaps and interest rate caps and collars.

(iii) The yield curve can be used to assess what the financial markets think the future movement in interest rates will be, and the size of those movements. Market expectations can be used by a company such as ours to make decisions about the balance between fixed rate and floating rate debt, or whether to fix future interest rates with a swap, interest rate futures or an FRA.

(e) **Credit risk**

Credit risk is the risk that a creditor will default, and be unable to pay a debt when it falls due for payment. For trading companies, credit risk is an unavoidable aspect of giving trade credit to customers. It can only be managed through efficient credit vetting and debt management policies and procedures.

(f) **Free cash flow**

A company needs cash to meet its payment obligations as they fall due. Cash can be obtained by borrowing, by issuing new shares, or by selling off assets. In the long run, however, a company should be able to generate sufficient cash from its operations to meet all its obligations and have some surplus cash to use at its discretion.

Free cash flow can be defined as the amount of cash a company has left over from its operations (ie from operational cash flow) for discretionary spending, after deducting essential items of cash spending. Essential spending will include interest payments on debt, payments of taxation and necessary capital spending (eg for regular replacement of fixed assets as they wear out). The surplus free cash flow might be used for discretionary new investment, or to pay out to shareholders as dividends.

If a company does not have any free cash flow, it will have to resort to measures such as borrowing or selling off assets to remain solvent and in business.

5 KILTER PLC

(a) A company should seek to minimise its overall cost of capital (its weighted average cost of capital) in order to maximise the total 'enterprise value' of the company. According to the fundamental theory of share values, the value of a company should represent the present value of all its future expected net cash flows, discounted at its weighted average cost of capital. The lower the discount rate, the higher the present value. When enterprise value is maximised, the wealth of the company's equity shareholders will also be maximised.

(b) Discussions about gearing and the cost of capital are based on the presumption that the cost of debt is always less than the cost of equity. This is partly because equity investors expect a higher return than on debt investments (to compensate for the higher investment risk) and partly because a company benefits from tax relief on interest payments, but not on dividend payments to shareholders.

The so-called 'traditional' view of capital gearing is that at low levels of gearing, any additional gearing does not have a big effect on the cost of equity. Consequently, as the gearing level rises, the weighted average cost of capital falls. However, as the gearing level rises still further, the perceived financial risk to equity investors increases. The cost of equity therefore rises, because equity shareholders now expect a return on their investment to compensate them for the higher financial risk. When the rising cost of

equity capital outweighs the benefits of more debt in the capital structure, the weighted average cost of capital starts to rise.

The traditional view of gearing is therefore that the weighted average cost of capital is minimised at an optimal mix of debt and equity, and a company should seek to achieve this optimal mix. In the case of Kilter plc, there is insufficient information to suggest whether a further increase in gearing would be likely to increase or reduce the weighted average cost of capital (assuming, of course, that the 'traditional' view of gearing and the cost of capital is correct).

The traditional view was challenged by Modigliani and Miller. Initially, they ignored taxation and the tax relief on debt interest, and argued that the weighted average cost of capital would be the same at all levels of gearing, and that the cost of capital is unaffected by the way in which the company is financed. If a company tried to reduce its cost of capital by taking on more debt finance and increasing gearing, they argued, the cost of equity would rise so as to leave the weighted average cost of capital the same as before. Any benefits from lower-cost debt capital would therefore be eliminated by the change in equity investor expectations.

Modigliani and Miller subsequently changed their views, to allow for the interest relief on debt capital. They then argued that as the level of gearing increased, the weighted average cost of capital would rise due to the tax effect. Consequently, a company should seek to maximise its gearing.

MM's arguments were based on certain simplifying assumptions. These included an assumption that the cost of debt itself is unaffected by a company's gearing level, except at very high gearing. In practice, the cost of borrowing goes up for heavily-indebted companies. MM also ignored the effect on the cost of equity and debt of bankruptcy risk and bankruptcy costs. In practice, when a company's debt levels become high, the risk of default increases and investors will demand higher returns accordingly.

It is therefore probable that, despite the carefully-argued logic of MM, the traditional view of the cost of capital and gearing is likely to apply, and a company could have an optimal gearing level that minimises the cost of capital and maximises enterprise value.

(c) The major factors affecting the amount of extra debt capital that Kilter might be able to raise will be as follows.

(i) **The perceived creditworthiness of the company**. If the company tried to obtain a bank loan, the bank would analyse its financial position carefully, and assess whether the company should be able to support the amount of debt it is asking for. If the company tried to raise money through a bond issue, credit rating agencies would perform a similar task. The credit assessment will have particular regard for the company's sales, profits and operating cash flows. A company with stable and steadily growing sales, profits and operating cash flows is much more able to support a large amount of debt finance than a company with volatile profits and cash flows.

(ii) **Cash flows**. Expected cash flows from the company's trading operations will also be an important consideration to would-be lenders. A lender will need to feel confident that the company should generate sufficient cash flows from its operations to meet all its interest payment obligations.

(iii) **Security**. A lender might demand security for any loan. The security could be in the form of a fixed charge over assets of the company, or a floating charge over the company's assets and the enterprise as a whole. Where security is demanded, the lender will want to be sure that it is sufficient. Kilter might therefore find it

difficult to raise a loan to finance the take over of a company with few assets, where the purchase price includes a large goodwill element.

(iv) **Borrowing restrictions.** The company might have restrictions on its ability to borrow. Although such restrictions could be imposed by the articles of association, or by company policy, the most common form of restriction arises from covenants on existing borrowing. Loan covenants might, for example, set a maximum limit to the borrower's gearing level, or might require the borrower to maintain its interest cover ratio above a specified minimum level. When a borrower breaches a loan covenant, it is technically in default, and the lender has the right, should it wish, to call in the loan immediately.

(v) **Lender perceptions of gearing and risk**. The amount that a company can borrow could vary according to perceptions in the financial markets about what levels of borrowing are 'tolerable'. The views of the markets have been known to change substantially over time. As an example, banks and bond investors lent considerable amounts of money to telecommunications companies in 1999 and 2000, only to take the reverse view, that telecommunications companies were far too heavily-geared, in 2001. New lending to these companies was therefore cut back severely, and interest rates demanded by bond investors rose sharply.

6 BLANK LIMITED

(a) (i) The cost of equity, using the CAPM, is 10% + 1.2 (15% – 10%) = 16%.

This cost of equity can now be applied in the dividend valuation model to find the total market value of equity. Since the company is all-equity financed, it is also the total value of the company. It is assumed that all earnings are distributed as dividend; earnings and therefore dividends will not grow. The current annual dividend, given no interest and a tax rate of 30%, is 70% of £400,000 = £280,000.

Value = Annual dividend/Cost of capital
= £280,000/ 0.16 = £1,750,000

The situation under the different scenarios can be summarised as follows.

	Current	*With 10% debentures*	*With 12% loan stock*
	£	£	£
Profit before interest and tax	400,000	400,000	400,000
Interest	0	50,000	120,000
	400,000	350,000	280,000
Tax (30%)	120,000	105,000	84,000
Earnings	280,000	245,000	196,000

According to the basic theory of capital structure developed by Modigliani and Miller, the market value of a firm is independent of capital structure. However, when tax is introduced into the calculations, the market value of the firm will increase as debt is added to the capital mix because of the present value of the tax shield on interest payments. This can be expressed as:

$$V_g = V_u + Dt$$

where
V_g = market value of the geared company
V_u = market value of the ungeared company
D = market value of debt
t = rate of corporation tax

In this case:

	Current	*With 10% debentures*	*With 12% loan stock*
Value of debt (D)	0	£500,000	£1,000,000
Tax rate (t)	0.3	0.3	0.3
	£	£	£
Value of ungeared company	1,750,000	1,750,000	1,750,000
Dt	0	150,000	300,000
Value of company	1,750,000	1,900,000	2,050,000

The value of the company's equity can now be calculated.

	With 10% debentures	*With 12% loan stock*
	£	£
Value of company	1,900,000	2,050,000
Value of debt	500,000	1,000,000
Value of equity	1,400,000	1,050,000

(ii) The ratio of debt to equity is given by D/E:

With 10% debentures	*With 12% loan stock*
500,000/1,400,000	1,000,000/1,050,000
= 0.36	= 0.95

(iii) Assuming that all distributable profits are paid as dividends, the cost of equity can be calculated as d/P where d is the annual dividend and P is the equity market value.

With 10% debentures	*With 12% loan stock*
245,000/1,400,000	196 ,000/1,050,000
= 17.5%	= 18.7%

(b) The contention that capital structure is irrelevant to the value of the firm was first put forward by Modigliani and Miller. Until that point the traditional view was that there is an optimal mix of debt and equity that minimises the weighted average cost of capital (WACC).

The key difference between these two approaches is related to the behaviour of the rate of return required by shareholders as the gearing level rises. The traditional view is that the cost of equity remains at a constant level at low levels of gearing, causing the WACC to fall as the gearing increases. Beyond a certain point however, the shareholders begin to demand a higher rate of return in compensation for the higher level of financial risk and the WACC begins to rise.

Modigliani and Miller showed that the value of the firm was determined by the income generated from its business activities, and that the way this income was split between the providers of capital was irrelevant. If the shares of two firms with the same level of business risk but different gearing levels were traded at different prices, then shareholders would move from the overvalued to the undervalued firm and adjust their level of personal borrowing through the market to maintain their financial risk at the same level. This arbitrage process would force the total price of the two firms to a common equilibrium value.

The above discussion would suggest that capital structure is irrelevant. However in practical terms this is not the case and other factors come into play.

(i) Both corporate and personal taxation distort the theory and can cause a bias in favour of debt into the capital structure.

(ii) It is increasingly common for covenants to be placed on loans, for example to restrict the level of dividend payments to prevent the capital base being run down and thereby increasing the risk of the lenders.

(iii) The nature of the company's asset base affects the capital structure. Companies with a high level of tangible assets find it easier to take on debt since they are able to offer better security for borrowing than firms with a high level of intangible assets, such as software firms.

(iv) Managers may have a preference for one sort of finance over another, for example a preference for retained earnings over debt finance and equity issues. A preference for retained earnings could be due partly to the transaction costs involved in raising the finance, but has also to do with the balance of ownership and control. The use of retained earnings causes the minimum disruption to the existing balance of control and is often preferred for this reason.

(v) The nature of the projected cash flows will affect the ability of the firm to raise debt. The greater the potential variability in the cash flows, the less easy it will be for the firm to borrow, because a lender would want the borrower to be able to meet debt payment obligations out of current annual income.

(vi) High interest rates will deter firms from taking on a high level of borrowing. On the other hand, when interest rates are low and the bond market is buoyant, large companies might take the opportunity to raise additional finance through low fixed rate borrowing, even though this could increase their gearing level substantially.

(vii) If the firm has significant international operations, it may need to take on loans denominated in foreign currencies in order to minimise its currency exposure.

(viii) There may be a clause in the Articles of Association that restricts the ability of the firm to borrow.

7 DRYSTONE PLC

(a) It is assumed that the market prices of the shares and debentures are quoted excluding dividend and interest. Since the WACC is to be calculated based on market values, the cost of reserves can be ignored.

Cost of equity. The dividend valuation model taking into account growth will be used.

$$r = \frac{d(1+g)}{P} + g$$

where:
r = cost of equity
d = annual level of dividends (current year)
g = annual rate of growth in dividends
P = market price of shares (ex div)

In this case: r = (4/80) + 0.12
= 0.17 or 17.0%

Cost of preference shares

$$r = \frac{d}{P}$$

$$r = \frac{9}{72}$$

= 0.125 or 12.5%

Cost of debentures. It is assumed that the debentures are irredeemable. The after tax cost to the company will be calculated.

$$r = \frac{d(1-t)}{P}$$

where t is the rate of corporation tax

$$r = \frac{14p(1-0.30)}{100p}$$

= 0.098 or 9.8%.

Weighted average cost of capital (WACC)

	Number/ Nominal value	*Price*	*Total market value*	*Cost of capital*	*MV × cost*
	000s		£000		
Equity shares	10,400	0.80	8,320	0.17	1,414.4
Pref shares	4,500	0.72	3,240	0.125	405.0
Debentures	5,000	1.00	5,000	0.098	490.0
			16,560		2,309.4

WACC = (2,309.4/16,560) = 13.95%

(b) The capital asset pricing model (CAPM) provides an alternative to the dividend valuation model as a method of calculating the cost of equity. Unlike the dividend valuation model, the CAPM seeks to differentiate between the various types of risk faced by a firm and to allow for the fact that new projects undertaken may carry a different level of risk from the existing business.

The model focuses on the level of systematic risk attaching to the firm, in other words, that element of risk which is common to all investments and which cannot be avoided by diversification.

The model uses the beta factor as a measure of an individual share's volatility of expected returns as against the market average. A beta factor of less than 1.0 indicates that the expected volatility is less than that of the market as a whole, and vice versa.

The model can be formulated as follows:

$$r = r_f + [r_m - r_f]\,\beta$$

where: r = cost of equity capital
β = beta factor for the firm
r_m = market rate of return
r_f = risk free rate of return

Thus the additional information that would be required is as follows.

Beta factor. This can be calculated statistically from historical records of:

(i) the returns earned by the share in terms of capital gains/losses and dividends
(ii) the overall returns earned by the market.

Market rate of return. The average annual rate of return on the securities market as a whole. This can be calculated from historical records.

Risk-free rate of return. This is generally taken to be the rate of return on government stocks.

(c) The net (after tax) payment made by the company on the debentures is:

£5m × 14% × 0.70 = £490,000

In order to raise the £5m through a preference share issue, the company would need to offer the shares at a price to yield 12.5% to investors. The annual cost in dividends would be 12.5% of £5m, ie £625,000.

Thus if preference shares are issued instead of debentures, annual equity earnings would be reduced by £135,000 (£625,000 – £490,000).

8 PUMP AND FLOW

(a) Since Pump plc has constant earnings all of which are distributed as dividends, the cost of equity can be estimated as d/P

where d = annual dividend

P = ex-div market value

Earnings available to be paid as dividends are as follows.

	£'000
Earnings before interest and tax	15,000
Interest (£24,000,000 × 16%)	3,840
	11,160
Tax at 30%	3,348
	7,812

$$\text{Cost of equity} = \frac{£7,812,000}{12,500,000 \times 100/25 \times 80p} \times 100\% = 19.53\%$$

The cost of debt can be estimated by comparing the current market value of the debt with the discounted payments due to be made by the company up to the redemption date. The interest cost per £100 of debt (nominal value) is £16. After tax relief, it is £11.20.

Year	*Cash flow* £	*Discount factor, 8%*	*PV at 8%* £	*Discount factor, 10%*	*PV at 10%* £
1	11.2	0.93	10.42	0.91	10.19
2	11.2	0.86	9.63	0.83	9.30
3	11.2	0.79	8.85	0.75	8.40
3	100.0	0.79	79.00	0.75	75.00
			107.90		102.89

Market value of debt = 104.17, which means that the actual cost of debt after tax is above 8% and below 10%. Interpolating:

$$\text{Cost of debt} = 8\% + \frac{107.90 - 104.17}{107.90 - 102.89} \times (10 - 8)\% = 9.49\%$$

The total market value of debt = £24 million × 104.17 = £25 million

	Market value £'000	*Cost*	*MV × Cost* £
Equity	40,000	0.1953	7,812.0
Debt	25,000	0.0949	2,372.5
	65,000		10,184.5

$$\text{WACC} = \frac{10,184.5}{65,000} \times 100\% = 15.67\%$$

(b) (i) Using Modigliani and Miller's theory, the market value will equal the market value of the company if it were wholly equity financed, plus the present value of tax relief on any debt interest:

$$V_g = V_u + Dt$$

where: V_g = total market value (D + E)
V_u = market value if equity financed
D = debt
t = tax rate

In this case:

$$V_g = £32.5m + (£5.0m \times 0.30)$$
$$= £34.0m$$

Since D = £5.0m
E = £29.0m

The market value of equity will decrease by £3.5m = (£32.5m – £29.0m).

(ii) The weighted average cost of capital (WACC) can be found as follows.

$$WACC = Ke_u \left[1 - \frac{Dt}{E+D}\right]$$

$$= 0.18 \left[1 - \frac{5 \times 0.3}{34.0}\right] = 17.2\%$$

The weighted average cost of capital has fallen by 0.8% (18 – 17.2%) due to the benefit of tax relief on debt interest payments.

(iii) $$WACC = [Ke_g \frac{E}{E+D}] + [K_d (1-t) \frac{D}{E+D}]$$

$$17.2 = [Ke_g \times \frac{29.0}{34.0}] + [13 \times (1-0.3) \times \frac{5}{34.0}]$$

$$15.86 = [Ke_g \times \frac{29.0}{34.0}]$$

$Ke_g = 18.6\%$

(c) MM theory is based on the assumption that the total market value of any firm is independent of its capital structure, and can be found by discounting its expected future returns at the cost of capital. It is based on the principle of arbitrage whereby it is assumed that investors are able to adjust their own level of personal gearing and are not reliant on companies in which they invest to do this for them. However, taken to its logical conclusion and taking into account taxation, the theory would recommend a capital structure wholly made up of debt.

Problems with the theory include the following.

(i) It ignores the possibility of bankruptcy at very high levels of gearing. As gearing rises, the cost of debt as well as the cost of equity will rise to compensate investors for the higher financial risk.

(ii) It assumes that companies can increase their gearing up to any level and ignores both the effect of restrictive covenants being imposed by lenders at high levels of gearing and the reality of the market.

(iii) It assumes that the company will be able to use all available tax relief on interest payments. As the gearing level rises this is less likely to be true in practice.

(iv) Taking these weaknesses into account, it would be expected that there is an optimal level of gearing which is below 100%, but there is no explicit method by which a company can determine what this optimal point or range might be.

9 NETRA AND BACKWOODS

(a) (i) The original value of Netra's shares is 2m × £4.20 = £8.4m.

If the company borrows £2m and redeems £2m of shares, the value of shares will be reduced by £2m but increased by the value of the tax shield Dt = £2m × 30% = £0.60m.

The capital structure in market values will therefore be:

	£m
Ordinary shares (E) (8.4 – 2 + 0.6)	7.0
Debt (D)	2.0
E + D	9.0

Similarly, if £4m is borrowed, the tax shield will be £4m × 30% = £1.20m and the capital structure in market values will be:

	£m
Ordinary shares (E) (8.4 – 4 + 1.2)	5.6
Debt (D)	4.0
E + D	9.6

The company's earnings before interest and tax are £2.5m. When the company is ungeared there is no interest cost, so tax is 30% × £2.5m = £0.75m and earnings after tax (available for ordinary shareholders) are £2.5m – £0.75m = £1.75m.

Assuming no growth in earnings, and that all earnings are paid out as dividends, the company's cost of equity capital is £1.75m/£8.4m = 20.83%.

Using Miller and Modigliani's model (with corporate tax) the company's weighted average cost of capital (WACC) at any other gearing ratio can be estimated from the formula:

$$WACC_g = K_{eu}(1 - \frac{Dt}{E+D})$$

When £2m is borrowed, $WACC_g$ = 20.83% [1 – (0.60/9.0)] = 19.44%.
When £4m is borrowed, $WACC_g$ = 20.83% [(1 – 1.20/9.60)] = 18.23%.

This illustrates the Miller/Modigliani theory that WACC decreases with increased gearing.

(ii) Although it is likely that WACC will fall as gearing is increased (provided the gearing level does not get too high), the estimates of WACC made in the above computations are subject to a high degree of error. This is due to the restrictive assumptions made by the Miller/Modigliani model and factors which it ignores.

These assumptions include a perfect capital market with no transactions costs, information which is costless and readily available, risk free debt and rational investors who all make the same forecasts of companies' results.

The two most important omissions from the theory are:

(1) **Personal taxation:** the theory allows for corporate tax relief on debt interest but ignores the fact that investors' equity returns are not taxed in exactly the same way as interest. Introduction of the personal taxation of investors into the theory is difficult (and different for every country) but has a material effect on the predicted cost of capital.

(2) **Insolvency risk:** in MM's theory, risk is measured entirely by volatility of earnings. The fact that earnings may be so bad that the company becomes insolvent is ignored. However, insolvency risk undoubtedly works to

increase the cost of both equity and debt at high levels of gearing, causing WACC to rise.

Other problems with the theory at high gearing are 'agency costs' (eg lenders impose restrictive covenants, causing a rise in the cost of equity) and 'tax shield exhaustion' (if taxable profits are zero, interest paid cannot produce any further reduction in tax).

(b) The discount rate that should be used is the weighted average cost of capital (WACC), with weightings based on market values. The cost of capital should take into account the systematic risk of the new investment, and therefore it will not be appropriate to use the company's existing equity beta. Instead, the estimated equity beta of the main German competitor in the same industry as the new proposed plant will be ungeared, and then the capital structure of Backwoods applied to find the WACC to be used for the discount rate.

Since the systematic risk of debt can be assumed to be zero, the German equity beta can be 'ungeared' using the following expression.

$$ß_a = β_e \frac{E}{E + D(1-t)}$$

where:

$ß_a$ = asset beta
$ß_e$ = equity beta
E = proportion of equity in capital structure
D = proportion of debt in capital structure
t = tax rate

For the German company:

$$ß_a = 1.5\left(\frac{60}{60 + 40(1-0.30)}\right) = 1.023$$

The next step is to calculate the debt and equity of Backwoods based on market values.

		£m
Equity	450m shares at 376p	1,692.0
Debt: bank loans		135.0
Debt: bonds	(75 million × 1.20)	90.0
Total debt		225.0

This can now be substituted into the capital asset pricing model (CAPM) to find the cost of equity.

K_e = rf + $[E(r_m) - r_f]\, ß_j$

where: K_e = cost of equity
r_f = risk free rate of return
$E(r_m)$ = market rate of return
K_e = 7.75% + (14.5% – 7.75%) × 1.023 = 14.65%

Then, re-gear at the company's gearing ratio, using MM:

$$WACC_g = K_{eu}\left[1 - \frac{Dt}{E + D}\right]$$

= 14.65 ×[1 – (225 × 0.30)/(1,692 + 225)] = 14.17%

10 DIVIDENDS

(a) The argument that dividend policy is irrelevant to the valuation of a company is based on the theory that a company's value is determined by the future expected earnings of the company, and the level of risk associated with the company. The company value is the present value of the expected future earnings, discounted at the cost of capital (which reflects the level of risk).

The argument states that it does not matter whether the earnings are paid out as dividends, or reinvested to achieve further dividend growth in the future. This can be shown mathematically, provided that it can be assumed that any earnings that are reinvested would obtain a return equal to the company's cost of capital. The loss in current dividends will be compensated for by the increase in the share price due to expectations of higher future earnings and dividends.

Modigliani and Miller, supporting the dividend irrelevance argument, suggested that individual shareholders can develop their own balance between current income and future growth, without having to rely on the dividend policy of the company. If a shareholder wants current income, and the company is not paying a dividend high enough to satisfy him, the shareholder can simply sell some shares in the stock market to obtain the additional income he wants. Similarly, if a shareholder would prefer earnings to be retained and a lower current dividend, he can use some of the dividend he receives to invest in additional shares in the company. Logically, therefore, shareholders should not value shares on the basis of the dividends that they expect the company to pay.

Another element of the argument is that a company should also be indifferent between paying out earnings as dividends or reinvesting the earnings (assuming that sufficient reinvestment opportunities exist). If it paid a high dividend and as a consequence needed extra finance to invest in profitable projects, it could simply raise the required extra finance by issuing new shares.

The MM argument assumed, however, that there is no taxation and no costs of buying or selling shares, and that there are no share issue costs. In practice, however, taxation can affect the preference for dividends or share price growth, and share transaction costs can deter shareholders from selling or buying shares to achieve a balance between income and reinvestment.

(b) Criticisms of the dividend irrelevance argument are largely focused on the simplifying assumptions in MM's arguments. In practice, shareholder preference for dividends or reinvestment for capital growth can depend on the differing tax treatment of dividend income and capital gains. In the UK for example, private individual shareholders receive a tax credit on dividend payments but are liable for income tax on the dividend; and they pay capital gains tax on any realised gains on their shares, subject to an annual exemption that is not taxed. It could therefore be more efficient for private shareholders to have dividends rather than capital gain, or vice versa, depending on their tax position.

It is also unrealistic to assume that there are no share transaction costs. The costs of using a stockbroker to buy or sell shares can be significant, especially for small transactions, and in the UK, stamp duty is payable on purchases of shares. Shareholders will therefore be reluctant to buy and sell shares to adjust their balance between income and reinvestment.

Share issue costs are high, and if a company needs to obtain finance for new investments, it will often prefer to obtain the money by retaining earnings rather than raising new capital in the market.

If the dividend irrelevance argument is correct, there is no such thing as an optimum dividend policy. The company's directors therefore need not concern themselves with dividends, which are a minor aspect of the financial management of the company.

On the other hand, if the dividend irrelevance argument is incorrect, and dividend policy is important to shareholders and the valuation they put on their shares, directors should give careful attention to finding an optimal dividend policy.

In practice, there are various reasons why the directors of a company might give careful thought to dividend policy.

(i) Dividends can act as a signal to investors in the stock market. For example, a company might increase its annual dividend, and the increase would signal the confidence of the directors in the future of the company and expectations for future profits. For similar reasons, the directors might decide to maintain current year dividends at the same level as the previous year, in spite of a fall in profits or even having to report a current year loss.

(ii) Shareholders often have expectations of the dividend policy of the company, and invest accordingly. For example, if a shareholder wants high annual dividends, he will invest in shares of companies that have a track record of a high dividend policy. Similarly, shareholders looking for a long-term investment and capital growth might opt for shares in companies with a track record of low dividends but successful investment and share price growth.

(c) Factors that will influence the amount of dividends that a company will pay include the following.

(i) Availability of cash. The size of a dividend a company can pay could be restricted by the amount of cash it has available to make the payment.

(ii) Availability of profits. A company is restricted by law from paying a dividend unless it has sufficient distributable reserves. Distributable reserves are, essentially, retained profits of the company, for the current and previous years.

11 XYZ PLC

(a) During the period 20X1 – 20X5, earnings per share have fallen by 11%, whereas the dividend per share has increased by 19%. The dividend cover has fallen from 1.7 times to 1.25 times. Assuming that the capital structure has not changed over the period, then it can be seen that actual annual earnings have declined over the period, and the amount of profits retained for reinvestment has fallen from £5.6 million in 20X1 to just £2.5m in 20X5. The expectation for 20X6 that if the dividend is maintained at the same level as in 20X5, the company will only just have enough earnings to meet dividends out of current year profits, and there will be no retained earnings at all.

A possible implication of this policy is that insufficient earnings have been retained to finance the investment required to continue with the development and growth of the company's business. If this means that the company is falling behind its competitors, then this could have a serious impact on the long-term profitability of the business.

Dividends can act as a signal to the stock market, and in the case of XYZ, it will not have escaped the notice of investors that the company has continued to increase dividends each year in spite of the decline in EPS. It is likely that the current share price will be sustained because of investors' expectations of continuing growth in the annual dividend income. However, it seems likely that the share price would now be much higher if some dividends had been reinvested to achieve earnings growth. In other words, share price growth might have been 'sacrificed' in order to pay the higher dividends.

(b) For the purposes of calculation, it is assumed that any new investment will earn a rate of return of 15%, which is equivalent to the return required by the shareholders. It is also assumed that a return of 15% will be maintained by the company's current investments into the foreseeable future. This means that the company will be able to maintain minimum annual earnings of £10,000,000 even if it pays out all its earnings as dividends in 20X6. Any dividends reinvested will contribute towards future dividend growth.

It is also assumed that investors are indifferent as to whether they receive their returns in the form of dividend or as capital appreciation. (In practice, however, this assumption is unlikely to be valid.)

Option 1

The amount of dividend per share is £1 with no growth forecast. The rate of return required by shareholders is 15%. The theoretical share price can be estimated using the dividend valuation model.

$$P = \frac{d(1+g)}{(r-g)}$$

where r = Rate of return on equity
d = Current year dividend per share
P = Market value per share, ex dividend
g = Growth rate per annum in dividend per share (as a proportion)

$$P = \frac{£1}{0.15}$$

P = £6.67 ex dividend, and including the current year's dividend of £1 per share, the value is £7.67

100% of the shareholders' return will be provided in the form of annual dividends. The annual dividend will be £6.67, which represents a return of 15% on a share with a market price of £6.67.

Option 2

In this case the current year dividend will be 50p and the remaining 50p of earnings will be reinvested at 15%. The annual growth rate in dividends will be g = rb, where r is the return on investment and b is the proportion of earnings retained. Here, $g = 0.15 \times 0.5 = 0.075$.

$$P = \frac{50(1+0.075)}{(0.15-0.075)}$$

P = 717p or £7.17

This price is (£7.17 – £6.67) = 50p higher than the share price would be if no profits were retained and all earnings were paid as dividend. With this dividend policy, 50% of the current annual return to shareholders (50p) is represented by dividend and the other 50p by share price growth.

Allowing for the current dividend receivable, the cum dividend share price is £7.17 + £0.50 = £7.67. This is the same as with option 1.

Option 3

The calculation is similar to the calculation for option 2.

$g = 0.15 \times 0.75 = 0.1125$

$$P = \frac{25(1+0.1125)}{(0.15-0.1125)}$$

P = 742p or £7.42

This price is (£7.42 – £6.67) = 75p higher than the share price would be if no profits were retained and all earnings were paid as dividend. With this dividend policy, 25% of the current annual return to shareholders (25p) is represented by dividend and the other 75p by share price growth.

Allowing for the current dividend receivable, the cum dividend share price is £7.42 + £0.25 = £7.67. This is the same as with options 1 and 2.

Option 4

In this case, the share value will be the present value of all future earnings, discounted at the cost of capital. The present value of these earnings, allowing for the current year earnings of £1 per share, will be £7.67 per share, the same as with options 1, 2 and 3. 100% of the expected return is provided in the form of capital appreciation under this option, with none of the return in the form of dividends.

The figures calculated above assume that the share price is wholly dependent on the rate of return required by shareholders, so that the share valuation can be estimated using the 'fundamental theory of share values'. It has also been assumed the shareholders, most of them private investors, are indifferent as to the whether the return is in the form of dividends or whether it comes as share price growth. This is unlikely to be the case.

(c) Other significant influences on dividend policy should be as follows.

(i) There might be funds available for investment from other sources (eg borrowing). The company could maintain a high dividend pay-out and still invest for growth if it is able to borrow or raise new equity capital by issuing new shares.

(ii) Investor confidence is important. Shareholders will be more supportive of a high dividend retention policy if they are confident that the company will achieve (or exceed) the target return on investment.

(iii) The income requirements of investors, and the taxation of dividend income compared with the taxation of capital gains, should influence the dividend policy. For example, if dividend income is taxed at a high rate and capital gains at a much lower rate, the company would be justified in a high dividend retention policy for share price growth. If shareholders needed income, they could sell some shares, and would pay capital gains tax rather than income tax on the money they obtain.

(iv) The availability of new investment opportunities that will provide the required rate of return is also significant. The company should not seek to reinvest if it is unable to obtain a return that is at least equal to the company's cost of capital.

The figures calculated are helpful to the directors in so far as they demonstrate that the share price is driven by expected earnings and dividends, dividend growth and the rate of return required by investors. Unless new investment is made, the share price will not grow (unless required returns also fall).

The directors should look in detail at the options available to them in terms of investment and assess these against the cost of capital, taking account of the differing degrees of risk entailed. For the share price to be maximised in the long term, it is the effect of investment policy on the net worth of the business which is important, ie the net present value of operating cash flows. This could mean that in the short term the share price declines, but this could be a worthwhile sacrifice to make for the long-term profitability of the business. The directors might also need to consider whether the company needs a further injection of capital in addition to an increase in dividend retention in order to fund its development.

12 POSTER PLC

(a) **Forecast earnings and dividends**

	Earnings	*Dividends*
	pence	pence
20X6 (20X5 figure plus 25%)	77.50	31.25
20X7 (plus 25%)	96.88	39.06
20X8 (earnings up 10%, divs 50% of earnings)	106.56	53.28
20X9 (plus 10%)		58.61

Dividend valuation model

The valuation of the company's shares is based on the assumption that the share price is the present value of all future dividends, discounted at the shareholders' required rate of return.

From 20X9 onward, the dividend growth rate will stabilise at 10% per annum. The present value of the shares as at the end of 20X8 will therefore be:

$$\text{Share price 20X8} = \frac{\text{Dividend at end of 20X9}}{(r - g)}$$

where r is the cost of capital (0.18) and g is the annual growth rate in dividends (0.10).

$$\text{Share price 20X8} = \frac{58.61}{(0.18 - 0.10)}$$

ie 733p

The current value of the shares is now calculated by discounting the 20X8 value and dividends in 20X6 and 20X7 back to a present (20X5) value.

Value at 20X5

Year		*Item*	*Amount*	*Discount factor at 18%*	*Present value*
			pence		pence
20X6	1	20X6 dividend	31.25	0.85	26.6
20X7	2	20X7 dividend	39.06	0.72	28.1
20X8	3	20X8 dividend	53.28	0.61	32.5
20X8	3	Share price ex div	733.0	0.61	447.1
					534.3

If the market accepts the forecast of the equity market analysts, the share price should rise to 534p. EPS in 20X5 were 62p. The P/E ratio as at the end of 20X5 would therefore be

P/E ratio = 534p/62p = 8.6 times.

The dividend valuation model includes a number of assumptions as follows.

(i) Future dividends will be of the same risk class as existing dividends.

(ii) Shareholders can be viewed as a homogeneous group, ie there are no variations in their information, attitude to risk and so on.

Its major weakness relates to the assumption that the level of business risk will not change as the firm develops and grows. If this assumption cannot be met then it might be more appropriate to use a different approach to valuation such as the capital asset pricing model.

(b) The company's dividend policy appears to have been one of maintaining a dividend cover ratio of around 2.5, which means that 40% of earnings each year are paid out in dividends. The share price has risen by nearly 50% over a four-year period. However, the P/E ratio has been fairly low throughout the period, and has not exceeded 6 at any time.

It is not clear what policy the company might have followed if earnings per share had fallen in any year. If the directors maintained a dividend cover ratio of around 2.5, they would have to cut the dividend in any year that EPS fell.

Other options available to Poster plc

The company could decide not to set a defined long-term dividend payout ratio but could instead make a review of its shareholders each year to decide what would be most appropriate and to follow the trends being set by other firms.

Instead of managing the payout ratio, the company could decide to try to maintain a constant real level of dividends regardless of the profit performance in an individual year.

The directors could decide not to make any dividend distributions at all and to use retained earnings as a major source of finance for new investments. In adopting this policy, the company would need to attract shareholders interested in capital growth rather than dividend income.

Note:

You might have suggested another dividend policy. For example, you could have suggested a higher dividend policy, with a lower dividend cover. The consequence of this policy would be lower share price growth over time, unless the company is able to raise more finance from other sources, eg in the form of debt capital.

13 SAND PLC

(a) **Share repurchase as an alternative to dividend payments**

If the surplus cash is distributed to shareholders as a dividend, this will result in a large percentage increase in dividend in the year of the payout. Shareholders will no doubt be happy with the cash received but, in the absence of further explanations, will become confused by what the company is trying to 'signal' by this dividend increase. Some investors may assume that further large increases in dividend can be expected in future years, and may develop over-optimistic expectations of the company's prospects.

Most finance directors take the view that it is best to increase dividends at a steady rate which signals the company's long-run growth prospects. If the board of directors agrees with this view, and wishes to make an above-average distribution to shareholders, it may consider using the balance of surplus cash to buy back some of the company's shares

In the UK, the Companies Act 1985 gives companies rights to buy back shares from shareholders who are willing to sell them, subject to certain conditions. The share buy-back requires provision in the company's Articles of Association and approval in

general meeting. It can be arranged as a series of purchases on the open market or as a private purchase from a number of large shareholders.

Share repurchases allow the company to make occasional distributions of surplus funds, without raising expectations of a sustained rise in annual dividend levels.

A share repurchase scheme has several other benefits.

(i) It is a way of using surplus cash that the company has no immediate use for. Invested cash yields a low rate of income (interest), far below the company's cost of capital.

(ii) By using cash to reduce the number of shares in issue, there will be some loss of earnings that would otherwise be obtained from bank deposit interest. However there should be an increase in the earnings per share, due to the reduction in the number of shares in issue. This could lead to a higher share price than would otherwise be the case.

(iii) If the company has a longer-term requirement for the cash, it can use a share repurchase scheme as an opportunity to increase its financial gearing. Repurchasing the company's own shares allows debt to be substituted for equity when finance is raised in the future. This could therefore be of interest to a company wanting to increase its gearing without increasing its total long-term funding.

(iv) Where a company is in decline or has gone 'ex growth', share repurchases will enable it to readjust the company's equity base to a lower, more appropriate level.

There are also possible disadvantages of a share buyback.

(i) It can be hard to arrive at a repurchase price that is fair both to the shareholders selling their shares and to any shareholders who are not selling their shares to the company. In principle, the buyback should be at the current market price, but the demand from the company to buy shares could drive up the market price, at least in the short term.

(ii) A purchase of shares could be seen as an admission that the company cannot make better use of the funds than the shareholders.

(iii) Some shareholders may suffer from being taxed on the capital gain arising on the repurchase of their shares rather than receiving dividend income.

(b) **Advisability of borrowing money to pay dividends in years 2 and 3**

Borrowing money to pay dividends is legal provided that the dividends are covered by the accumulated distributable profits of the company. The question, however, is whether such a course of action is financially advisable.

In theory, if cash is invested and dividends are reduced, this should not worry shareholders provided that they can see the prospect of increased future dividends. In practice, for 'signalling' reasons mentioned above, it is commonly believed that shareholders are happiest when they receive a steady stream of dividends increasing from year to year.

This is an argument in favour of borrowing in order to maintain the dividend growth. Shareholders receive more cash in years 2 and 3 but less in future years because of the need to repay the loans with interest.

Given that the company is not highly geared (debt: equity ratio of 1:5) the company probably has sufficient borrowing capacity to borrow as much as is needed to maintain dividend growth in line with long-term earnings growth. This course of action might therefore be adopted by the board of Sand plc.

(c) **Effect on the company's cost of capital**

If shares are repurchased, the total value of equity should go down by the amount of cash paid out while debt remains unchanged. This will result in an increase in gearing. The cost of equity will rise because of the increased financial risk (volatility of equity earnings) experienced by the shareholders.

In the same way, if the company increases its borrowings in order to pay dividends, the gearing will increase and the cost of equity capital will rise.

However, Sand plc is operating at a low level of gearing. The increase in the cost of equity is likely to be outweighed by the cheap after-tax cost of debt compared with equity. The tax savings resulting from debt interest will mean that, even though the cost of equity goes up, the weighted average cost of capital will be reduced. This should result in a higher value for the enterprise and a higher equity value per share for the remaining shareholders.

14 LIME PLC

(a) Interest rate exposure arises when a company's borrowing is such that a change in interest rates might expose it to interest charges that are unacceptably high. For example, if a company has a large tranche of debt at a fixed rate of interest that is due for repayment in the near future, and the loan is to be replaced or renegotiated, the company would be vulnerable to a sudden increase in market interest rates.

Risk management in this context involves using hedging techniques to reduce or 'cover' an exposure. However, hedging has a cost, which will either take the form of a fee to a financial institution or a reduction in profit, and this must be weighed against the reduction in financial risks that the hedge achieves. The extent to which the exposure is covered is known as the 'hedge efficiency'. A perfect hedge has an efficiency of 100%.

Methods of managing interest rate risk include the following.

Forward interest rate agreements (FRAs)

An FRA is a contractual agreement with a bank, about the interest rate on a future notional loan or deposit. The agreement fixes the rate of interest for borrowing at a certain time in the future. If the actual rate of interest at that time is above that agreed FRA rate, the bank pays the company the difference, and vice versa. An FRA is simply an agreement about rates. It does not involve the movement of the principal sum; the actual borrowing must be arranged separately. The FRA receipt or payment, taken with the actual interest payable on the loan itself, in effect fixes the interest rate for the borrower. However, although the company benefits from effectively fixing the rate of interest on a loan for a given period, it also misses the opportunity to benefit from any fall in interest rates below the FRA rate during the contract period.

Futures

A financial future is an agreement on the future price of a financial item, such as a notional three-month deposit. Interest rate futures are similar to FRAs, except that the terms, sums involved, and periods are standardised. They are traded on futures exchanges. Futures in short-term sterling interest rates, for example, are traded on LIFFE. A borrower can hedge against the risk of a rise in interest rates by selling interest rate futures. Their standardised nature makes them less attractive to corporate borrowers because it is not always possible to match them exactly to specific interest rate exposures. Each contract sold or bought will require the payment of a small initial deposit, or margin.

Interest rate options

An interest rate guarantee (or option) gives its holder the right to borrow a specified notional amount for a specified time at a guaranteed rate of interest. The option has the effect of providing a guarantee to the option holder that the interest rate will not rise above a specified level during a specified period. On the date of expiry of the option the buyer must decide whether or not to exercise the option. He will only exercise the option if the actual interest rate has risen above the option strike rate. The advantage of interest rate options is that the buyer cannot lose on the interest rate and can take advantage of any favourable rate movements. However, a premium must be paid regardless of whether or not the option is exercised. Borrowers' options can be negotiated directly with a bank. Options on interest rate futures are also traded on futures exchanges.

Caps and collars

Caps are a series of borrowers' options, covering a number of consecutive interest periods. They can be used to set a ceiling to the interest rate for borrowing. As with any other type of option, a premium is payable by the buyer of a cap, and caps can be expensive. A collar is a cheaper form of instrument. Like a cap, it fixes an effective maximum interest rate, but it also fixes a minimum 'floor' borrowing rate too.

Swaps

An interest rate swap is an arrangement whereby two companies, or a company and a bank, swap interest rate commitments with each other on a notional amount of principal. A coupon swap can be used by a company to convert a fixed rate interest liability into a variable rate liability, or vice versa. Swaps are therefore used to manage the balance in a company's debt financing structure between fixed and floating rate interest, without having to renegotiate the underlying loan transactions, or without having to redeem bond issues or make new bond issues. Swaps can sometimes be used to arrange borrowing at a lower interest cost (through 'credit arbitrage').

(b) The cash flow estimates show that the company might be cash positive or cash negative at the end of month 3, and a cash investment decision should therefore be for just the next two months.

The company has £200,000 available to invest for up to two months now. In one month, it will have an additional £400,000 (probability 0.4) or £600,000 (probability 0.6) to invest for one month.

The options are:

Option 1. Invest £200,000 now for one month, and then invest either £600,000 or £800,000 for a further month from the end of month 1.

Option 2. Invest £200,000 now for two months, and then invest either £400,000 or £600,000 for one month from the end of month 1 to the end of month 2.

Option 1		*EV*
		£
Interest		
On £200,000 for 1 month at 6.5%	(£200,000 × 1/12 × 6.5%)	1,083
On £600,000 for 1 month at 6.8%	(£600,000 × 1/12 × 6.8% × 0.4)	1,360
On £800,000 for 1 month at 6.8%	(£800,000 × 1/12 × 6.8% × 0.6)	2,720
		5,163
Transaction costs	£150 + £200	(350)
Net receipts		4,813

Option 2		*EV*
		£
Interest		
On £200,000 for 2 months at 6.6%	(£200,000 × 2/12 × 6.6%)	2,200
On £400,000 for 1 month at 6.8%	(£400,000 × 1/12 × 6.8% × 0.4)	907
On £600,000 for 1 month at 6.8%	(£600,000 × 1/12 × 6.8% × 0.6)	2,040
		5,147
Transaction costs	£150 + (0.4 × £150) + (0.6 × £200)	(330)
Net receipts		4,817

Both options have about the same expected value. This suggests that the company should be indifferent as to which option it should choose.

15 CENTRALISATION AND RISK DATA

(a) (i) **What it means**

Centralisation of treasury management means that most decisions on borrowing, investment of cash surpluses, currency management and financial risk management will be taken by an enhanced central treasury team, based at head office, instead of by subsidiaries directly. A central treasury could take all surplus cash from subsidiaries and invest the surplus centrally. Similarly, a central treasury might do all the borrowing for the group, and lend money on to the subsidiaries. The subsidiaries would deal in matters of borrowing, lending and aspects of cash flow management with the central treasury, not with local banks and local capital markets. In addition, a central treasury department might be given the responsibility for setting most transfer prices for inter-company goods and services centrally.

(ii) **The potential benefits**

The main benefits are as follows.

(1) **Netting off inter-company debts before settlement.** At the moment, the company will be spending too much on foreign exchange commission by settling inter-company debts in a wide range of currencies through the banking system.

(2) **Knowledge of total group currency exposure from future currency transactions.** A central treasury can make greater use of hedging by matching revenues and payments in the same currency. Debtors in one foreign subsidiary can hedge creditors in a subsidiary in a different country, eliminating unnecessary hedging with forward exchange contracts by subsidiaries.

(3) **Knowledge of the group's total cash resources and borrowing requirement.** A central treasury can use its knowledge of the total group position on borrowing and lending by subsidiaries throughout the group. This knowledge could be used to reduce the incidence of one company lending cash while a fellow subsidiary borrows at a higher interest rate. Alternatively, a central treasury can insist that all loans and deposits by subsidiaries are made with the central treasury itself. Matching loans and deposits can reduce net interest payments for the group as a whole, and will eliminate unnecessary interest rate hedging. It will also facilitate higher deposit rates and lower borrowing rates, because the central treasury can negotiate better rates for larger loans or deposits.

(4) A reduction in the group's tax charge could be possible by means of a comprehensive centrally-set **transfer pricing policy.** The treasury department could apply transfer prices that will minimise total tax liabilities for the group, for example by 'moving profits' from countries with a high tax regime to countries where tax rates are lower.

(5) Enhanced control over financial risks will be possible because a central treasury will be able to develop a central team of specialists who will have a clear-cut strategy on hedging and risk management.

(iii) **Potential problems for subsidiaries and their solution**

The group culture is one of decentralisation. However, a centralised treasury will take decisions about funding and risk management away from subsidiaries and centralise them. In addition, centrally-determined transfer prices will have an impact on the profits of each subsidiary.

However, head office will also be taking away responsibilities that involve time and an understanding of financial risk management. This should give the management of subsidiaries more time to concentrate on planning and operational performance.

A centralised treasury system can only work properly if information exchange between head office and subsidiaries is swift and efficient. Enhanced computer systems should be provided at all foreign centres to assist with daily reporting. It is also important that the management of subsidiaries should keep the treasury department informed of all local conditions that could be beneficial to the treasury function, such as the availability of local subsidised loans, as well as potential local risks such as the threat of exchange control restrictions.

Decisions made by the treasury department that affect a subsidiary's profitability, such as transfer price decisions, and transferring surplus cash to head office, should be allowed for when assessing the performance of business units.

(b) To: Board of directors
From: Financial adviser
Date:

Subject: The evaluation of political risk in investment decisions

(i) **The measurement of political risk**

Political risk in foreign investment could be defined as the threat that a foreign government will change the rules of the game after the investment has been made. There are various agencies that can provide risk scores for different countries, but the key problem for all such approaches is that the scores that they use will always be subjective.

Considering the data that is being used in this case in more detail, there are a number of weaknesses that should be recognised.

1 Economic performance is one of the most heavily weighted factors. However it can be argued that this is not really a component of political risk.

2 There is no information as to how the weightings have been arrived at.

3 A number of factors that could have been included have been ignored. These include:

- Cultural homogeneity
- Quality of the infrastructure (transport systems etc)
- Legal system
- Record on nationalisation of private companies
- Currency stability

The directors should possibly consider some of the other approaches to the evaluation of political risk. These include:

1 Seeking the views of individuals with direct experience of the countries in question, such as academics, diplomats and journalists

2 Social as well as economic analysis.

(ii) **The decision about which country to invest in**

The evaluation of political risk must obviously form some part of the decision about which country to invest in. However, the use of this type of data to evaluate political risk in this context can be misleading for the following reasons:

1 These scores are valid at the 'macro level', but they do not measure the risk that is faced at the operational level by the industry or firm. Certain industries, such as mining and agriculture, are more prone to political risk than are others. Some activities will be welcomed by countries due to the perceived benefits that their presence can bring.

2 It can lead to an over-emphasis on the political features of the host country while neglecting other vital considerations such as the strategic fit of the new investment with the company's other operations.

Political risk data has relevance to the investment decision, but should not form the sole basis on which the decision is made. Although Forland comes out best in the overall scores, it has the worst level of economic performance. If the subsidiary is being developed with a view to serving primarily the local market, then this factor should receive a higher weighting in the overall decision making process since it will have a significant impact on the expected cash flow that will be generated.

16 TREASURY MANAGEMENT

(a) A central treasury department will normally have the responsibility for the management of the group's cash flows and borrowings. Subsidiaries with surplus cash will be required to submit the cash to the treasury department, and subsidiaries needing cash will borrow it from the treasury department, not from an external bank.

A central treasury will also be given the responsibility for borrowing on behalf of the group. If a subsidiary needs capital to invest, the treasury department will borrow the money required, and lend it on to the subsidiary. The subsidiary will be responsible for paying interest and repaying the capital to the treasury department, which will in turn be responsible for the interest and capital payments to the original lenders.

Another function of the treasury department will be to manage the financial risk of the group, such as currency risk and interest rate risk. Within broad guidelines, the treasurer might have authority to decide on the balance between fixed rate and floating rate borrowing, and to use swaps to adjust the balance. The department would also be responsible for arranging forward exchange contracts and other hedging transactions.

The central treasury department could also be responsible for the tax affairs of the group, and an objective would be to minimise the overall tax bill. To accomplish this effectively, the treasury must have authority to manage transfer prices between subsidiaries in the group, as a means of transferring profits from high-tax countries to lower-tax countries.

(b) There are no official or exact definitions of business risk and market risk, and the terms are used differently according to context. However, business risk arises from the sensitivity of cash flows, profits and asset values to changes in business conditions or circumstances. Examples of business risk would be a shortfall in revenues below the expected level, or unexpectedly high expenses, perhaps due to changing economic circumstances or actions by competitors, or due to changes in the situation facing the industry as a whole. Credit risk might also be included within business risk: this is the risk that customers will fail to pay debts they owe to the company.

Market risk arises from the sensitivity of cash flows to changes in conditions in the financial markets, such as a change in a key exchange rate or a rise or fall in interest rates. There is also a risk of changes in market conditions, such as when the equity markets, bond markets or loan markets 'dry up' and it becomes extremely difficult to raise long-term capital. For companies holding investments in shares or government bonds, market risk also arises from the possibility of a rise or fall in the stock market or bond market.

An important feature of risk is that it affects the sensitivity of cash flows to changes. When risk is higher, cash flows are more sensitive to unexpected variations, up or down. A function of treasury management is to control the risks, so that the company will be able to deal with any situation that arises. The tasks will involve:

(i) Identifying business and market risks.

(ii) Where appropriate, hedging currency risk and interest rate risk exposures. For example, currency risk can be reduced by matching revenue and spending in each currency, and through forward exchange contracts or foreign currency borrowing, or possibly currency derivatives.

(iii) Arranging borrowing for the group, and monitoring the financial risk in the company's gearing structure.

(iv) Arranging standby borrowing facilities.

(v) Planning and controlling the group's cash flow.

The management of credit risk will remain with the accounting function in each subsidiary.

(c) The treasury function needs information from within and from outside the organisation to carry out its tasks.

(i) From each subsidiary within the group, it will need figures for future cash receipts and payments, making a distinction between definite amounts and estimates of future amounts. This information about cash flows will be used to forecast the cash flows of the group, and identify any future borrowing needs, particularly short-term and medium-term requirements. Figures should be provided regularly, possibly on a daily basis.

(ii) Information will also be required about capital expenditure requirements, so that long-term capital can be made available to fund it.

(iii) Subsidiary finance managers should be encouraged to submit information to the treasury department about local market and business conditions, such as prospects for a change in the value of the local currency, or a change in interest rates.

(iv) From outside the group, the treasury will need a range of information about current market prices, such as exchange rates and interest rates, and about which banks are offering those prices. Large treasury departments will have a link to one or more information systems such as Reuters and Bloomberg.

(v) The treasury department should be alert to any favourable market opportunities for raising new debt capital. The treasurer should maintain regular contact with several banks, and expect to be kept informed of opportunities as they arise.

(vi) Where the treasury is responsible for the group's tax affairs, information will also be needed about tax regulations in each country where the group operates, and changes in those regulations.

(d) Business and market risk are concerned with potential consequences for cash flow and profit. In the short term, cash flow and liquidity are more important than profit. The treasury department is responsible for monitoring cash flows, and ensuring that if there will be insufficient cash flows from operations, other sources will be available to meet the company's payment obligations.

A cash budget is a useful starting point, because it allows the treasury team to take a medium-term view of cash requirements. However, for control purposes, the cash budget should be revised regularly, possibly daily, so that it reflects current expectations.

When an up-to-date forecast suggests that cash flows are unlikely to be sufficient, decisions can be taken for dealing with the problem, such as arranging short-term borrowing, or delaying payments to suppliers.

Exposures to risk can also be managed with a view to placing a cash flow limit on the maximum tolerable risk.

17 EXCHANGE RATES

(a) (i) Interest rate differentials explain the difference between spot exchange rates and forward rates. They are used for setting forward exchange rates in the foreign exchange markets. In this example, banks are able to quote a two-year forward rate for the dollar against sterling from current spot rates and current money market interest rates.

At the current spot rate (December 20X4) £1,000,000 in sterling has an equivalent value to $1,524,000.

£1 million could be invested now for two years at 5.75% per year to earn £1,000,000 × (1.0575) × (1.0575) = £1,118,306.

Alternatively, $1,524,000 could be invested now for two years at 6.5% per year to earn $1,524,000 × (1.065) × (1.065) = $1,728,559.

To the financial markets, £1,118,306 in two years has the same value as $1,728,559 in two years. The two-year forward exchange rate will therefore be: ($1,728,559/£1,118,306) = $1.55 approx. If this were not the forward rate, it would be possible to make arbitrage profits in the currency and money markets until rates adjusted.

Interest rates and interest rate differentials determine forward exchange rates, but they are only one factor in predicting future spot rates. Future movements in the spot rate are uncertain, and cannot be predicted now with certainty.

The non-executive director's comment that future spot rates can be predicted from interest rates is based on 'interest rate parity theory', but this is based on the supposition that other factors, such as the future rate of inflation in each country, will not affect the exchange rate. This is not the case. The fact that Superbank is forecasting a spot rate in two years of 1.55 is either coincidental, or based on an assumption that all other factors influencing exchange rates will be the same for both currencies (which is unlikely).

(ii) The wide spread of forecasts by the banks must be due to completely different assumptions made by each bank about the future influences on the value of each currency. The influence of the interest rate differential has already been discussed.

Other influences on the exchange rate will be as follows.

1 The rate of inflation in each country. If country X has a higher rate of inflation than country Y, the value of the currency of country X will be expected to weaken over time against the currency of country Y. This is because the currency of the country with a higher inflation rate is losing its 'purchasing power' in real terms. An exchange rate adjustment is therefore needed to maintain the purchasing power parity between the two currencies.

2 The balance of payments could influence the exchange rate. When a country exports less than it imports, it has a balance of payments deficit that must be financed by capital inflows, possibly foreign borrowing. A balance of trade deficit can have the effect of causing a currency to weaken.

3 However, international flows of capital now have a much greater influence on the value of currencies such as the dollar and sterling. When foreign investors want to invest in a country, the demand for the currency rises, and the currency strengthens in value. The sterling/dollar exchange rate will therefore be strongly affected by the investment situation and the economic outlook in each country.

Of the three forecasts by the banks, two indicate that the dollar will weaken and one that it will strengthen against sterling. Presumably, their views about inflation and the investment and trading outlook in each country vary widely.

(b) (i) The following are advantages of forward exchange contracts for the exporter.

1 It can fix an amount of sterling income that it will receive from the export transaction, and so can predict with certainty the profit or loss it will make on the transaction.

2 It will also know exactly how much money it will receive, and so can forecast its cash flows with greater accuracy.

3 Selling dollars forward provides a 100% hedge against the risk of a fall in the value of the dollar between the date of making the transaction and the date of eventually receiving the dollar income. Forward exchange contracts are an important instrument for hedging currency risk for both exporters and importers.

(ii) Assuming the company enters into forward contracts to sell dollars to his bank at 1.4900 in one month and 1.4840 in three months it will receive the following amounts in sterling.

	£
Now (spot): \$60,000 at \$1.4920	40,214.48
In one month: \$45,000 at \$1.4900	30,201.34
In 3 months: \$45,000 at \$1.4840	30,323.45
	100,739.27

(iii) Without hedging, the company would have received:

	£
Now (spot): \$60,000 at \$1.4920	40,214.48
In one month: \$45,000 at \$1.4960	30,080.21
In 3 months: \$45,000 at \$1.5040	29,920.21
	100,214.90

Since the spot value of the dollar has declined, the company will receive about £526 less. Depending on the size of the profit margin on the export transaction, this could have a significant effect on the company's trading profit.

(iv) Transactions in currency futures are available on some future exchanges. The CME trades futures for the dollar against sterling. Currency futures are very similar in concept to forward exchange contracts, the main difference being that futures contracts are standardised exchange-traded instruments and are not tailored to the specific needs of someone wanting to buy or sell currency. Currency futures are therefore used mainly for large currency transactions, for example by banks. The use of currency futures by trading companies is uncommon, certainly outside the US.

18 CURRENCY

(a) (i) Since the forward rate for the riyal against the \$A is lower than the spot rate, the implication is that the Saudi Arabia interest rate is lower than that in Australia. This is based on the interest rate parity theory, which states that in equilibrium the difference in interest rates between two countries is equal to the difference between the forward and the spot rates.

(ii) The Saudi Arabia interest rate can be estimated as follows.

Day 1	1 riyal buys spot	0.4825 \$A
Day 90	Interest at 5.5%	0.0066 \$A (0.4825 × 5.5% × 90/360)
	Total value	0.4891 \$A

This is now worth 1.0118 riyals (at A\$/SR 2.0687). Ninety-day interest is therefore 0.0118 riyals on a deposit of 1 riyal.

The annualised Saudi interest rate is therefore (0.0118 × 360/90) = 4.72%.

If the forward rate were SR/A\$ 0.4795, the forward A\$/SR rate would be (the inverse of this) 2.0855. The calculations would be as follows.

Day 1	1 riyal buys spot	0.4825 \$A
Day 90	Interest at 5.5%	0.0066 \$A
	Total value	0.4891 \$A

This is now worth 1.0200 riyals (at A\$/SR 2.0855). Ninety-day interest is therefore 0.0200 riyals on a deposit of 1 riyal.

The annualised Saudi interest rate would therefore be (0.02 × 360/90) = 8.0%

If the interest rate in Saudi Arabia is 5%:

A\$1 has a spot value of SR 2.0725.

A\$1 could be invested for 90 days at 5.5%, to earn interest of (1 × 5.5% × 90/360) A\$0.01375. The total value of the investment after 90 days would be A\$1.01375.

Similarly, SR 2.0725 could be invested for 90 days at 5%, to earn interest of (2.0725 × 5% × 90/360) = SR0.0259. The total value of the investment after 90 days would be SR2.0984.

The 90-day forward rate should therefore be:

2.0984/1.01375, ie A$/SR 2.0699.

This is the same as 1.01375/2.0984, ie SR/A$0.4831.

(b) (i) The Hungarian subsidiary will be incurring costs for raw materials and management charges in sterling. It will be receiving income from sales denominated in HUF and other central and eastern European currencies. If the HUF weakens against sterling, this will make its raw material and management costs relatively more expensive. At the same time, if the HUF weakens against other central and eastern European currencies, this will make its exports to these areas relatively cheaper. The weakening HUF will also mean that remittances to the UK will be subject to exchange losses for the UK parent.

One of the most effective ways of hedging is 'structural hedging'. This approach to covering currency exposures is to ensure as far as possible that assets in a particular currency are matched by liabilities in the same currency. In addition, income in a particular currency should be matched as far as possible by expenditures in the same currency. By transferring production to Hungary, the company is improving the extent to which matching is achieved, since a significant proportion of the labour costs as well as other expenses are now denominated in local currency. However, there is still likely to be some imbalance between income in forints and expenditures in the same currency. The company will also still be incurring a large amount of its costs in sterling.

In terms of financing the venture, relatively few assets need to be acquired locally. The decision on whether to lease or buy the buildings will depend on the relative costs of the different options, the availability of funds, and the relative costs of borrowing in the UK and in Hungary. However, it is likely that some form of lease will be appropriate since this will allow the company to retain flexibility as well as providing another opportunity for the matching of receipts and payments denominated in HUF.

(ii) The company has a number of options available to it in detailed terms when it comes to hedging its exposure to a weakening of the HUF. Specific techniques include the use of forward exchange contracts, if the size of the transactions are known in advance with reasonable certainty. It might also be possible to buy currency options (to sell forints in exchange for sterling) although these will be expensive if the forint is a weak currency.

19 CURRENCY EXPOSURE

(a) Likely future movements in the sterling/Freimark exchange rate should be considered. If it could be predicted that changes in the exchange rate were very likely to be favourable, there would be little point in protecting the group against risk. However, as the rate has been very volatile in the past, it is unlikely that such a prediction can be made. Some protection against future adverse currency fluctuations is almost certainly desirable, to protect the group against currency losses.

Expected future cash flows, beyond the next six months, should also be considered. It may be that there will be a clear trend in net receipts or payments, which can be taken account of in devising a currency exposure hedging strategy.

The position of any other companies in the group might give opportunities for protection. If other companies in the group have business denominated in the Freimark or in any other currencies that move in line with the Freimark, receipts by one company might be netted off against payments by another.

The group's approach to risk should be considered. It may be that potential currency losses are not large enough to be of real concern, or that the directors prefer to take risks of currency losses to have the chance of favourable currency movements and high rewards. On the other hand, the directors may prefer to take every opportunity to minimise risk, particularly if the potential losses could have a significant impact on group profits, if future currency movements are adverse.

(b) **Three techniques of exposure management**

(i) The company could open a Freimark bank account in the UK, possibly making an initial deposit so as to avoid having an overdraft in months 2 and 3. All transactions would be conducted through this account. Any planned withdrawals for conversion into sterling could be protected by forward exchange contracts. In the next six months, the receipts in FM and the payments in FM will roughly be the same amounts in total, so the bank account can be used, with an overdraft facility, to match payments and receipts in the same currency.

(ii) Forward exchange contracts could be entered into for each of the next six months. For example, the company could contract with a bank now for the conversion of FM 2,400,000 into sterling at the end of month 1, at a pre-arranged rate. As the cash flow forecasts may prove to be inaccurate, forward option contracts may be appropriate. These are binding contracts, but with some flexibility as to the completion date.

(iii) The company could use leading and lagging. This involves timing receipts and payments so as to take advantage of exchange rate movements. For example, if a payment in Freimarks is required, the currency should be bought and the payment made when sterling is strong against the Freimark.

(c) **Economic exposure is** the risk that the value of a business and its competitiveness will suffer through the impact of exchange rate movements on its future cash flows. It is a longer-term exposure than transaction exposure. Transaction exposure is specific to individual transactions and so tends to be short-term in duration. In contrast, economic exposure may affect the prosperity of a business into the longer-term future.

A company may be affected by longer-term exchange rate movements in several ways, particularly in global markets. If a company has a centre of operations in a country with a strong currency, its competitive position in foreign markets will suffer if the domestic currency strengthens, because rival suppliers producing in a different currency will become relatively cheaper. Foreign competitors will also become more price-competitive in the company's domestic markets. However, imports will be cheaper, as will future capital investment overseas.

Global companies need to consider ways of hedging economic exposures. One way of doing this is to re-locate operations into countries where the currency risk is lower, for example by establishing a production facility for the US markets in a country whose currency is linked to the value of the dollar.

20 PARTISAN PLC

To: Chief Executive
From: Financial Manager
Date

Report on the company's currency risk management policy

This report compares the company's existing foreign exchange risk management policy with alternative approaches.

(a) **Purposes of hedging foreign exchange risk**

Our company sells world-wide, invoicing for most transactions in the currency of the foreign country (the 'local currency') rather than in pounds sterling (the 'home currency'). Some of our foreign suppliers also invoice in their local currencies. Sales transactions may suffer from exchange losses, if the local currency weakens between the date of the contract and the date of cash settlement. Likewise, exchange losses on purchases can be made when foreign currencies strengthen.

The purpose of hedging is to limit or eliminate these exchange losses on transactions. Our company arranges a suitable hedge for all transactions worth £100,000 or more.

The main hedging technique we use is the forward foreign exchange contract. A forward contract is an agreement made in advance for the purchase or sale of a quantity of currency at a future date, at a fixed rate of exchange which is agreed in advance. A forward contract takes all risk out of the transaction, by fixing a certain rate for the exchange of currencies.

The company also uses the money markets for some currency hedging. For example, the company might expect to receive €1,000,000 in six months' time. Instead of arranging a forward contract to exchange the euros into sterling, we could borrow euros now and convert them into sterling. In six months, the receipt of the €1 million would be used to repay the loan with interest. This provides both a currency hedge and earlier cash receipts from the transaction.

The advantages of the hedging policy are that the cash flows for all material foreign currency transactions are predictable, exchange losses are eliminated and cash planning is made easier because of this.

The disadvantages are comparatively small for a risk-averse company. The main argument against hedging currency exposures is that potential exchange gains are eliminated along with the losses. In the year to 30 September 20X8, hedging eliminated £778,000 of foreign exchange losses, but in 20X9 potential exchange gains of £347,000 were forgone. When it seems probable that a particular currency is going to weaken, or that a currency is going to strengthen, it might be worth taking the risk, on suitable transactions, and not arranging a hedge. Instead of fixing an exchange rate now, the company could hope to obtain a better spot rate at a future date.

However, Partisan plc is a trading company, and it should seek to make the bulk of its profits from trading, and should not expose itself to excessive risks by 'gambling' on currency movements.

(b) **Financial implications of hedging the purchase of machinery**

Whereas the UK sales price for this machinery is fixed at £300,000, the purchase price depends on how the Hong Kong dollar moves against the pound sterling over the next three months. At today's forward rate of 11.2589, the company can be sure that its purchase cost will be £244,251, giving a trading profit of £55,749.

For the purpose of illustration, assume (1) that the HK$ weakens in three months time to 11.8800. If the company did not arrange a forward transaction, and bought the HK$ at the spot rate to pay the supplier, the supplier's invoice would be settled by a payment of £231,481. This would give a total profit on the transaction of £68,519.

However, if we assume (2) that the HK$ strengthens to 10.9900, and the exposure is not hedged by a forward contract, the payment will be £250,227. This will result a net profit of only £49,773.

(c) **Factors to consider before changing currency risk management policy**

Factors in favour of reducing the amount of hedging by means of forward contracts and money market transactions are as follows:

(i) Because we import and export, there will be instances where receipts and payments in the same currency can be matched, reducing the requirement for hedging, because any losses on the imports will be offset by gains on the exports, or vice versa. Even if the transaction amounts and dates do not match exactly, the amount, duration and cost of hedging can be significantly reduced by planning along these lines. The arrival of the euro has greatly increased our opportunities for matching payments on foreign imports and receipts from exports. 'Structural hedging' of this kind will be made easier by opening bank accounts in our major trading currencies, and arranging an overdraft facility on these accounts.

(ii) Because we trade in many countries world-wide, there could be a 'portfolio effect' or 'swings and roundabouts' effect. If we are exposed in many currencies, there is a possibility that sterling will strengthen against some currencies and weaken against others. Losses on some currency exposures could be offset by gains on other exposures. If the company took the view that gains and losses on currency exposures will offset each other, it might decide that hedging exposures is unnecessary.

(iii) Although many short-term currency movements are unpredictable, there are various factors which cause longer term movements. For example, if there is high inflation in a country from which we are purchasing, the currency is likely to devalue, and there will be little sense in always hedging against purchase transactions for that country.

Against these arguments are the following points.

(i) Although currency losses may be offset by gains in the longer run, the 'embarrassment factor' of a significant loss in any one year might cause customers to lose confidence in our management ability.

(ii) In extreme cases, currency losses might threaten the company's ability to continue in operations. Sudden dramatic realignments of exchange rates are not uncommon and, although predictable with hindsight, can take firms by surprise and cause huge losses.

(iii) For very large transactions, even small currency movements can create significant losses. It is wiser to hedge these transactions (assuming that matching cannot help) even if losses are not predicted.

The company's attitude to risk needs to be evaluated. The consequences of making currency losses, compared with the advantages of gains, need to be debated from the viewpoint of both the company as a whole and the individual managers involved. For transactions that cannot be matched, the alternative to our existing policy is not necessarily to abandon hedging altogether, but to develop a policy which takes into

account both predicted currency movement and the size of the transactions involved. It is possible that the threshold figure of £100,000 ought to be increased.

(d) **Alternative methods of managing currency risks**

As indicated above, the preferred technique for managing currency risk is to match receipts and payments in the same currency. This is conveniently done by opening a bank account in that currency. The company should consider opening bank accounts in several major currencies (eg euros, US dollars, Japanese yen and possibly in other freely-exchangeable currencies such as the Hong Kong dollar).

Progressing this argument, we should also think more about trying to match both sides of our import-export transactions in the same currency. For example we may be able to pay a German supplier in US dollars and sell the product to the USA, invoicing in dollars. We should also consider sourcing more products from those countries for which our sales are highest.

When financing our working capital, we should not necessarily be limited to loans in pounds sterling. For example, if our main assets (debtors) are mainly designated in US dollars, we should consider borrowing in dollars to offset the currency risk.

21 WEFT PLC

(a) (i) **Method 1**

Weft plc borrows €750,000.

Three months interest is €750,000 × 3% × 3/12 = €5,625.

The customer pays €750,000 in three months' time, which is sufficient to repay the loan principal but not the interest. The interest must be paid by converting pounds into euros. Since the amount of interest payable is known in advance, the euros can be purchased on the forward market at a cost of 5,625/1.5935 = £3,530.

The borrowed €750,000 will presumably be converted into sterling at the spot rate of €1.6006, to obtain £468,574. This money will be used somehow. Using the information available, it will be assumed that the company can invest the money at the sterling three-month interest rate of 5%.

Interest earned will be £468,574 × 5% × 3/12 = £5,857.

So, at the end of three months, the net sterling cash from the transaction is:

£468,574 + £5,857 – £3,530 = £470,901.

Method 2

The exchange rate is fixed in advance at €1.5935 by the forward contract. Cash received in three months is converted to produce €750,000/1.5935 = £470,662.

Conclusion

On the basis of the above calculations, Method 1 gives a slightly higher receipt. However, the difference is quite small, and banker's commission has been excluded from the calculation.

(ii) **Factors to consider before deciding whether to hedge foreign exchange risk using the foreign currency markets**

The company should have a clear strategy concerning how much foreign exchange risk it is prepared to bear. A highly risk-averse or 'defensive' strategy of hedging all transactions can be expensive in terms of commission costs, but recognises that exchange rates are unpredictable, can be volatile and so can cause severe losses unless the risk is hedged.

An alternative 'predictive' strategy recognises that if all transaction exposures are hedged, the chance of making gains from favourable exchange rate movements is lost. It might be possible to predict the future movement in an exchange rate with some confidence. The company could therefore attempt to forecast foreign exchange movements and only hedge those transactions where losses from currency exposures are predicted. For example, if inflation is high in a particular country, its currency will probably depreciate, so that there is little to be gained by hedging future *payments* in that currency. However, future receipts in a weak currency would be hedged, to provide protection against the anticipated currency loss.

A predictive strategy can be a risky strategy. If exchange rate movements were certain, speculators would almost certainly force an immediate fall in the exchange rate. However, some corporate treasurers argue that, if predictions are made sensibly, a predictive strategy for hedging should lead to higher profits within acceptable risk limits than a risk-averse strategy of hedging everything. Fewer hedging transactions will also mean lower commission costs payable to the bank. The risk remains, though, that a single large uncovered transaction could cause severe problems if the currency moves in the opposite direction to that predicted.

A sensible strategy for a company could be to set a maximum limit, in money terms, for a foreign currency exposure. Exposures above this amount should be hedged, but below this limit a predictive approach should be taken or, possibly, all amounts could be left unhedged.

Before using any technique to hedge foreign currency transactions, receipts and payments in the same currency at the same date should be offset. This technique is known as matching. For example, if the company is expecting to receive €750,000 on 31 March and to pay €600,000 at about the same time, only the net receipt of €150,000 needs to be considered as a currency exposure.

Matching can be applied to receipts and payments which do not take place on exactly the same day by simply hedging the period and amount of the difference between the receipt and payment, or even by using a currency bank account. A company that has many receipts and payments in a single currency such as the euro should consider matching assets with liabilities in the same currency.

(b) If the foreign subsidiary is selling its output predominantly in its own country, the principle of matching assets and liabilities suggests that the subsidiary should be financed as far as possible in the currency of that country. Ideally, the subsidiary will be highly geared with loans and overdrafts in the developing country's currency.

If local finance has not been used and the sales invoice in question is for a large amount, the company should take out a short-term loan in the currency and convert this into sterling at the spot rate. The loan should be repaid out of the eventual currency receipt.

If it is impossible to borrow in the local currency, Weft plc should attempt to find a 'hard' currency whose exchange value has a high positive correlation with the local currency. For example, some countries have a policy of pegging their currency to the US dollar. The receipt can then be hedged by selling the US dollar forward.

This technique is, however, open to the risk that the local currency suddenly devalues against the dollar. The likelihood of this happening is high if the country's economy gets into serious difficulties.

If Weft plc is fairly certain that the local currency is going to depreciate in value and that it cannot borrow in that currency, the remaining alternatives are:

(i) Increase the sales price by the amount of the expected devaluation and bear the currency risk.

(ii) Invoice in a hard currency, for example US dollars, which can then be sold forward.

(iii) Arrange a 'counter-trade' agreement. Counter-trade is a form of barter in which the sale of an exporter's products to a country with a weak currency is paid for in local raw materials or other products. These are then sold elsewhere to obtain hard currency.

22 GAUNT LTD

(a) Most interest rate swaps are coupon swaps. A coupon swap is an agreement between two parties, typically for a period of several years, to swap payments of interest on a notional principal amount. One party pays a fixed rate of interest on the principal, and the other pays a floating rate, such as LIBOR.

A company might want to borrow at a fixed rate of interest, but might be too small to issue fixed-rate bonds. In such a situation, it could borrow from a bank at a floating rate of interest and use a coupon swap to 'convert' the floating rate interest liabilities to an effective fixed rate liability.

An interest rate swap could be useful to a rapidly-growing company because:

(i) the company is likely to need to borrow to finance its growth, and

(ii) it might want to obtain fixed rate funding so that its future interest payment obligations are known with certainty.

Swaps would therefore help the company to reduce the uncertainty about its future interest rate costs.

Occasionally, it might be possible to obtain a lower effective interest rate by means of a swap. For example, a company wishing to borrow at a fixed rate might be able to borrow more cheaply by borrowing at a floating rate and arranging a swap than by borrowing directly at a fixed rate.

In a currency swap, a similar transaction is agreed between the two parties, except the nominal principal is in two currencies. For example, a company might arrange a currency swap with a bank in which it pays interest on a nominal amount of principal in currency A, and receives interest on an equivalent amount of nominal principal in currency B. At the end of the swap, they must then exchange the principal amounts. For example, a company might arrange a four-year currency swap where the principal amounts are £10 million in sterling and US$15 million. The company might receive interest on the sterling at a fixed rate, and pay interest on the dollars at a fixed rate. At the end of the swap, the company would then receive £10 million and pay $15 million.

For a company that is starting to trade internationally, and uses debt finance, a currency swap can be used to create payment obligations in the currency of a country where the company is exporting to. For example, if a UK company is selling goods to the US, it can arrange a swap in which it pays US dollars and receives sterling. In this way, by creating US dollar payment obligations, it can match the US dollar receipts from its exports with the swap payments (at least in part) and so reduce its currency exposures.

A further advantage could be that if the interest rate in the other currency is lower than in sterling, it will be able to obtain lower interest expenditure, without actually having to borrow in the foreign currency.

Both interest rate swaps and currency swaps are easy to arrange, at least in the major trading currencies. They are also flexible, since they can be arranged in any size and are reversible. The only transaction costs incurred are legal fees and there is no commission or premium to be paid.

If staff in the company have little experience of international finance, then it may be more appropriate for them to begin by using some of the simpler hedging instruments such as forward exchange contracts, before moving on to more complex procedures such as currency swaps.

(b) (i) The company's present policy is to arrange forward contracts. These fix the future sterling cost of payments in yen, and eliminate the risk of a large movement in exchange rates (ie appreciation in the yen against sterling) before the payments become due. The company therefore knows what its future commitments are going to be. On some occasions, with the benefit of hindsight, the company would save money by waiting to arrange the purchase of yen and buying at spot when the funds are required. This would happen if the yen were to depreciate in value. However, by not arranging forward contracts, the company has currency exposures and runs the risk that the yen will appreciate in value.

(ii) The suggestion of buying yen now and placing them on deposit will not save the company any money. This is because forward exchange rates reflect interest rate differences between the currencies. This can be illustrated with the figures quoted by the managing director. Suppose for example that the company has to pay 10 million yen in one year's time. With interest at just 0.10%, the company would need to put (10 million/1.001) 9,990,010 yen on deposit now for one year to have the 10 million yen available after one year to make the payment. These yen would cost the company (999,010/174.82) £57,145 to buy at the spot rate. This amount of sterling could be deposited and invested at 4.5%, to become £59,717 with interest after 12 months (£57,145 × 1.045). By arranging a forward contract to buy 10 million yen at 167.51 in 12 months, the sterling cost would be £59,698. This could be paid for by the sterling on deposit. These calculations show that there is no benefit at all in the managing director's second suggestion.

(iii) By borrowing in yen to pay off sterling loans, the company would be increasing its yen liabilities and reducing its sterling liabilities. It seems likely that the company will therefore be creating an exposure to the yen. The interest rate payments on the yen would be very low, but it is quite likely that the yen will strengthen in value against sterling over time. The cost in sterling of meeting the interest rate payments and eventually repaying the yen loan will therefore increase over time. The benefit of the low interest rate on the yen should therefore tend to be cancelled out by an appreciation in the value of the yen.

The company might take the view that the yen will not appreciate so much, and that the interest rate on the yen is not indicative of the likely future movement in the exchange rate. If so, there could be a financial advantage in borrowing in yen. However, such a course of action would give the company a large exposure to currency risk.

23 BAILEY SMALL

(a) (i) Since both the receipts and payments are expected to occur on the same date, Bailey Small plc need only hedge the net amount, ie a receipt of \$200,000 (\$450,000 – \$250,000). To hedge this transaction, a three-month forward contract to sell dollars will be required. The rate that will apply for this contract will be \$1.6590 – \$0.0077 = \$1.6513.

The transaction cost will be paid immediately in US\$. It is 0.2% of \$200,000, ie \$400. Bailey Small must therefore buy dollars now to cover this at the spot rate of \$1.6540.

The net receipt is as follows:

	£
Sterling proceeds in 3 months' time: \$200,000/1.6513	121,117
Transaction cost: \$400/1.6540	(242)
Net receipt	120,875

(ii) Since the company is expecting to receive dollars, to effect a money market hedge it will need to borrow dollars now in anticipation. The sum to be borrowed must be just enough so that the receipt in three months' time will repay the loan and the interest due for the period.

The money will be borrowed in dollars at an annual rate of 6%. This equates to a three-month rate of 1.5% (6%/4). The amount to be borrowed in dollars is therefore \$200,000/1.015 = \$197,044. These dollars will be sold now at the spot rate of \$1.6590 to realise £118,772.

This sterling amount can now be invested in the UK at an annual rate of 6.5%. This equates to a three-month rate of 1.625%. The value of the deposit at the end of the three month period when the dollar loan is repaid will be £118,772 × 1.01625 = £120,702.

The transaction cost will be the same as for the forward market hedge. The net receipt under this method will therefore be £120,702 – £242 = £120,460.

The receipts are highest if the forward market hedge is used, and this will therefore be the preferred method, although the net income difference between the two methods is not large.

(b) A fixed forward exchange contract is:

(i) An immediately firm and binding contract (between a bank and its customer)

(ii) For the purchase or sale of a specified quantity of a stated foreign currency

(iii) At a rate of exchange fixed at the time the contract is made

(iv) For performance at a future time which is agreed upon when making the contract

An option forward exchange contract has many of the features of a fixed contract. It is an agreement for the exchange of a specified quantity of one currency in exchange for another at a future date, at a rate of exchange agreed when the option is bought. The key difference is that the option buyer has the right to call for performance of the transaction, and is not obliged to carry out the transaction. An option will therefore only be exercised if it is to the option holder's benefit to do so.

Currency option contracts could be attractive when there is uncertainty about the likely movement, up or down, in the exchange rate. The option buyer, in this case the company, can take advantage of any favourable movements in exchange rates, while continuing to hedge any unfavourable movements.

A significant drawback to buying option contracts are that they are more expensive than fixed forward contracts, since the premium has to be paid, whether or not the option is exercised. They are traded in standard amounts, and it is therefore difficult to hedge exactly the sum required. In practice, this means that the company will have to carry some of the risk itself.

Bailey Small example

The company is expecting a net receipt of dollars and so is exposed to the risk of a fall in the value of the dollar against sterling. The hedge should therefore be arranged to give the company a worst-possible exchange rate. This can be achieved by purchasing call options on sterling.

The cash flow will be at the end of June, so the company will need to buy June call options.

The spot rate for selling dollars is currently \$1.6590. If the dollar weakens and the rate falls below the current spot rate, the company will benefit from the movement in rates. The strike prices to consider are \$1.65 and \$1.70. A strike price of \$1.65 is slightly in the money, and is more expensive than an option with a strike price of \$1.70.

The company might select to buy options at \$1.70. These will be exercised if the spot rate goes above \$1.70 by June.

The sum to be hedged is \$200,000. The amount of sterling that needs to be purchased is therefore \$200,000/1.70 = £117,647. At £12,500 per option contract, the number of contracts required is (£117,647/£12,500) 9.4 contracts.

The company should therefore buy nine contracts, giving it the option to buy £112,500 at \$1.70, for \$191,250. It is assumed that it will bear the remaining risk itself (which is \$200,000 - \$191,250 = \$8,750).

The option premiums will be payable immediately, and it is assumed that dollars will be bought now at spot to cover this. The cost is:

(9 × 12,500 × \$0.017) = \$1,912.50, and at a spot rate of 1.6540, the cost in sterling is £1,156.

The option will only be exercised if the spot price is more than \$1.70. If we assumed that the spot rate moves to, say, \$1.71, the options would be exercised and net receipts for the company from the \$200,000 would be as follows:

	£
Nine contracts of £12,500	112,500
\$8,750 sold at spot (1.71)	5,116
Less premium (above)	(1,156)
	116,460

If the spot price actually moved to that predicted in the question, the option would not be exercised and the company would sell the dollars on the spot market at \$1.6513. The net receipts would be as follows:

	£
\$200,000 sold at \$1.6513	121,116
Less premium (above)	(1,156)
	119,960

The actual spot rate happens to be the forward rate that the company could have secured in March. In this example, the company is therefore 'worse off' by the amount of the premium it paid to buy the options, less the transaction cost on the forward contract.

Given the actual movement in exchange rates that occurred, it can be seen in retrospect that Bailey Small's best decision would have been to have used a fixed forward contract rather than an option, since this would have yielded a receipt of £120,875 (greater than £119,960).

However, had the dollar fallen further against sterling, for example, to $1.60, then hedging with options would have yielded a greater receipt than the fixed forward contract. At this exchange rate, the options would not be exercised and the net receipt would be as follows:

	£
$200,000 sold at $1.60	125,000
Less premium	(1,156)
	123,884

The key point is that the option contract gives the company a hedge against unfavourable exchange rate movements but at the same time allows the possibility of benefiting from unexpected favourable movements in rates. The 'correct' choice can only be made once the company has specified the degree of risk that it is willing to accept in this type of situation.

24 BRIE SA

(a) **Transaction exposure** is the risk of adverse exchange rate movements occurring in the course of normal international trading transactions. The exposure arises when a transaction involving a currency exchange will be made or settled at a future date. The exposure arises because there is a risk of an adverse movement in the exchange rate between 'now' and the transaction settlement date.

A transaction exposure arises for example when an exporter sells goods in a foreign currency, for settlement at a future date, or when an importer purchases goods priced in a foreign currency, for payment at a future date.

Transaction exposures can give rise to real cash flow gains and losses, due to favourable or adverse movements in the exchange rate. It is therefore an important function of treasury management to assess the risk and manage it where appropriate, using hedging instruments such as forward exchange contracts or currency derivatives.

Translation exposure arises from differences in the currencies in which assets and liabilities are denominated. If a company has different proportions of its assets and liabilities denominated in particular currencies, then exchange rate movements are likely to have varying effects on the value of these assets and liabilities. For example, a company might have all its assets in sterling, but a loan in US dollars.

A translation exposure arises from the risk that when the value of the foreign currency assets or liabilities are translated into the company's domestic currency, for the purpose of financial reporting, gains or losses will arise from one year to the next due to changes in the rate of exchange at which the foreign currency assets or liabilities are translated.

These effects occur when consolidated group accounts are prepared, and the reporting parent company has foreign subsidiaries.

The importance of this form of exposure to the financial manager stems from the fact that this could influence investors' and lenders' attitudes to the financial worth and creditworthiness of the company. Such risk can be reduced if assets and liabilities denominated in particular currencies can be held in balanced amounts, so that the group's total assets in any foreign currency are roughly equal to its liabilities in the same currency. Unlike transaction exposure, translation exposure is effectively an accounting measure and is not reflected in actual cash flows. This means that hedging techniques (other than 'structural hedging' to balance assets and liabilities in a foreign currency) are not normally relevant.

(b) Since the receipt and payment are expected to arise at the same time, it is only necessary to hedge the net payment that will be required of \$2.8m (\$7.6m – \$4.8m) in three months' time. The methods available are the forward market and currency options.

Using the forward market, the company would buy \$2.8m three months forward at €/\$1.0715.

The cost of this is \$2.8m × 1.0715 = €3,000,200.

(c) **Using currency options**

Dollars are being purchased in three months' time. The company wants to protect itself against an increase in the value of the dollar and a fall in the value of the euro in the next three months. Option strike rates are rates for the price of the euro against the dollar. Since the company wants protection against a fall in the value of the euro, put options will be purchased.

At \$/ €0.938, the exchange value of \$2.8m = (2.8m/0.938) €2,985,075.

With a contract size of €62,500, the company must purchase (2,985,075/62,500) 48 contracts.

The premium cost is 62,500 × 48 × 1.57 cents = \$47,100

This is payable now, and will cost in euros \$47,100 × 1.0661 = €50,213.

(d) If the exchange rate on 15 September is \$/\$0.9700, the options will not be exercised. The company will buy the €2.8 million at the spot rate.

The overall cost for the company will be:

	€
Cost of \$2.8m at €/\$0.9700	2,886,598
Cost of option premiums	50,213
	2,936,811

This gives an effective \$/€ exchange rate of (2,936,811/2.8 million) \$/ €1.0489. In this particular case, hedging with options has been a lower-cost method of hedging the currency exposure than arranging a forward exchange contract.

25 BLUNT PLC

(a) The non-executive director is concerned with the foreign exchange exposure which arises on the translation of assets denominated in foreign currencies on consolidation. The most effective way to reduce this when the foreign currency is depreciating is to minimise the value of the net assets denominated in the currencies in question, ie to match assets denominated in a foreign currency as much as possible with liabilities in the same currency. The effects of the hedging proposals are likely to be as follows.

(i) The **early collection of foreign currency receivables** will not affect translation exposure, because the foreign subsidiary will simply be receiving cash (an asset) from its debtors (also an asset). Early collection of foreign currency receivables is a form of hedging transaction exposures, when the receivables are immediately converted into the company's domestic currency on receipt. This does not appear to be what the non-executive director has in mind in this case.

(ii) The effect of **early foreign currency loan repayments** will have the opposite effect to what the non-executive director appears to have in mind. Repaying foreign currency loans will increase the group's net assets in foreign currency, and so increase the size of its translation exposure.

However, if a currency loan is in a currency that is appreciating in value against sterling, there might be an argument for repaying these loans early. However, much would depend on the interest rate payable on the loans. Interest rates tend to be lower on appreciating currencies.

(iii) A **reduction in the stock level** will reduce the risk of translation exposure since it will reduce the level of net assets. However, such a reduction should not be at the expense of operating efficiency and competitive position in the subsidiary.

Although the advice to reduce translation exposure will improve the appearance of the group's accounts, it must be appreciated that such a loss is different from transaction exposure since it is not a *realised loss*. It is only an accounting loss, arising because of the nature of financial reporting.

In terms of the share price, if the stock market is efficient and shares are priced on the basis of the earning potential of the assets, a reported loss on translation of foreign subsidiaries' net assets should have little effect on the market position of the shares.

(b) **Multilateral netting** is a procedure whereby the debts of the different group companies denominated in a given currency are netted off against each other. The principal benefit is that foreign exchange purchase costs, including commission, the buy/sell spread and money transmission costs are reduced. Additionally there is less interest lost since money spends less time in transit. Blunt plc would be able to net as shown in the table below.

	Paying company						
	UK	*1*	*2*	*3*	*4*	*Total rec'd*	*Net receipts/ (payments)*
Receiving company	$000	$000	$000	000	$000	$000	$000
UK		300	450	210	270	1,230	(470)
1	700		420		180	1,300	220
2	140	340		410	700	1,590	380
3	300	140	230		350	1,020	(110)
4	560	300	110	510		1,480	(20)
Total paid	1,700	1,080	1,210	1,130	1,500	6,620	0

Although dollar payments amounting to $600,000 will still need to be made by the UK and countries 3 and 4 to countries 1 and 2, these amounts are small in comparison with the total value of transactions which amounts to $6.62m.

26 PLANKTON PLC

(a) (i) At current exchange rates of around £/€1.58, the size of the deal equates to approximately £63m. This is a large amount to borrow from a single bank, although it is possible that the loan could be arranged through one of the largest German banks. However, for a loan of this size the arrangement could be spread across a number of banks, in a syndicated loan arrangement. This would also have the advantage of spreading the risk of default.

An advantage of borrowing from banks is that the details of the loan arrangements will not be made public, and the company will not have to obtain a credit rating for the debt.

A disadvantage of borrowing from the German banking system is that the loan arrangement will be subject to German law and jurisdiction, and this could give rise to practical difficulties. For example, if the company were to default on the loan agreement, the banks might pursue the matter through the German legal system, which Plankton's management might know little about.

A further problem with bank borrowing, compared to borrowing by issuing bonds, is that the banks could require security in the form of a charge over the assets of the company. Bonds, in comparison, are usually unsecured.

The loan covenants and warranties could also be more stringent than for a bond issue, although this is not certain to be the case.

(ii) If Plankton elects to use the eurocurrency market, it could raise a loan in euros (possibly a syndicated loan) through the international banking system, probably at a floating rate of interest.

The advantages and disadvantages of eurocurrency borrowing are much the same as for borrowing in the domestic banking market. However, a eurocurrency loan could be arranged through a UK lead bank, and made subject to the law and jurisdiction of England and Wales.

(b) (i) **Summary of swap transactions**

The current spot rate (mid rate) is (1.5790 + 1.5806)/2 = 1.5798. Plankton wants to borrow €100 million, which is equivalent to (100 million/1.5798) £63.3 million. In the cross-currency swap arrangement, Plankton will issue bonds with a nominal value of £63.3 million, and pay interest at 7% per year. The annual interest cost would be £4,431,000.

In the swap, the German company would pay interest at 7.5% on notional principal of £63.3 million, ie interest of £4,747,500.

Plankton will therefore make an annual gain in sterling of (£4,747,500 - £4,431,000) = £316,500 from the sterling cash flows.

Plankton will also pay interest at euribor + 1% to the German company on notional principal of €100 million.

At the end of the swap in three years' time, the German company will pay £63.3 million to Plankton, and Plankton will pay €100 million euros to the German company. These payments can be used to redeem the bond issue (in the case of Plankton) and the bank loan (in the case of the German company).

The swap could be of potential benefit to both Plankton and the German company as a means of reducing their overall borrowing costs. The potential benefit is shown in the table below, although the interest rates make no distinction between the currencies of the cash flows.

	Plankton	*German company*
	%	%
Actual borrowing	(7%)	(Euribor + 1.5%)
Swap payments and receipts		
Pay	(Euribor + 1%)	(7.5%)
Receive	7.5%	Euribor + 1%
Net cost of borrowing	(Euribor + 0.5%)	(8.0%)

If Plankton were to enter into the currency swap, it would receive a fixed rate of interest from the German company of 7.5% per year, which represents a net benefit of 0.5% (7.5% – 7%),over the interest cost of the bonds. At the same time it would pay the German company at euribor + 1.0% per year. The alternative

would be to borrow directly at euribor + 0.75% per year. Thus the swap offers Plankton a gain compared with direct borrowing of 0.25% per year, although this is a gain of 0.5% per year in sterling and an extra cost of 0.25% in euros. Against this must be offset any fee to the bank that arranges the swap transaction.

(ii) The benefits of swaps include the following.

(1) The companies may be able to structure the timing of payments so as to improve the matching of cash outflows with revenues.

(2) The companies gain access to debt finance in another country and currency where it is little known, and consequently has a poorer credit rating, than in its own country.

(3) The swap provides a hedge against currency risk for the full five-year period.

(4) Swaps give companies the opportunity to restructure their interest rate liabilities in terms of the relative proportions of fixed rate and floating rate debt, without the need to restructure the debt base itself.

The disadvantages of swaps include the following.

(1) There is the risk of one of the parties defaulting, since the bank arranging the swap will not in this case act as the counterparty in two legs of the swap. The agreement appears to be directly between Plankton and the German company.

(2) There is the risk that interest rates and exchange rates could move in such a way that the net payments arising as a result of the swap are higher than they would have been had the swap not been undertaken.

27 EUNOMIA LTD

Workings: floating rate loan

Interest rate in first quarter =		8%
Interest rate in second quarter =	(0.8 × 10%) + (0.2 × 5%) =	9%
Interest rate in third quarter =	10% plus or minus 2.5%, ie 7.5% or 12.5%, or 5% plus or minus 2.5%, ie 2.5% or 7.5%	

Probabilities:
(0.8 × 0.5) = 0.40 prob of (10% + 2.5%) 12.5%
(0.8 × 0.5) = 0.40 prob of (10% - 2.5%) 7.5%
(0.2 × 0.5) = 0.10 prob of (5% + 2.5%) 7.5%
(0.2 × 0.5) = 0.10 prob of (5% - 2.5%) 2.5%

EV of expected interest rate =
(0.40 × 12.5%) + (0.40 × 7.5%) + (0.10 × 7.5%) + (0.10 × 2.5%) = 9%

(a) **Expected cost**

Fixed rate agreement		£
Interest	8.5% × £400,000 × 9/12	25,500
Issue costs	1.5% of £400,000	6,000
		31,500

Floating rate agreement		£
1st quarter interest	8% × £400,000 × 3/12	8,000
2nd quarter interest	9% × £400,000 × 3/12	9,000
3rd quarter interest	9% × £400,000 × 3/12	9,000
Issue costs	2% of £400,000	8,000
		34,000

On the basis of these figures, the fixed rate loan option appears to be cheaper. However, the figures for the floating rate option are based on an expected value of the interest rate in each quarter, and the actual interest costs could be either much higher or much lower, depending largely on whether the interest rate rises or falls for quarter 2.

On the balance of the estimated probabilities, the fixed rate option is cheaper, However, it might be worth reviewing the estimates of future interest rate movements before making a final decision.

(b) The method of hedging interest rate risk will depend on the term of the loan. For short-term borrowing, FRAs or borrowers' options might be suitable. For longer-term borrowing, an interest rate swap or a long-term option (a cap or a collar) would be suitable.

It is assumed in this solution that longer-term hedging is required.

Interest rate swap

The company can enter into a coupon swap agreement with a bank at any time. If the company wishes to hedge the risk of a rise in interest rates, it would want to lock in a fixed rate of interest payments before interest rates actually rise. It can do this in a swap by arranging to be the payer of the fixed rate of interest and to receive a floating rate of interest (usually LIBOR). The swap would be for a notional amount of principal equal to the amount of the variable rate loan for which the hedge is required. Payments under the swap agreement can be arranged to occur at the same time as the interest payments on the loan.

Suppose for example that the company pays floating rate interest at LIBOR plus 1%. By entering into a swap agreement to receive LIBOR and pay a fixed rate of F%, the net result would be for the company to pay an effective fixed rate on its borrowings of (F + 1)%.

A swap can be arranged for the same term as the company's floating rate loan. Should the company wish to change its decision at any time, and start to pay a floating rate again, it can either negotiate a cancellation of the original loan agreement, or make yet another swap agreement.

A cap or collar

An interest rate cap is a series of borrowers' options, for which the exercise dates can be timed to coincide with interest payment dates under the loan agreement. A cap gives its holder the right, but not the obligation, to borrow a notional amount of principal for each of a succession of interest periods, at a fixed rate of interest (the strike rate for the cap). The amount of the notional principal should be the same as the amount of the company's floating rate loan. If, at an exercise date for the cap, the actual benchmark rate of interest is higher than the strike rate, the option will be exercised. If the benchmark rate of interest is lower than the strike rate, the option will be allowed to lapse.

When an option is exercised, the option writer must make a payment to the option holder, based on the difference between the strike rate of interest and the current benchmark rate. This compensation payment offsets the higher interest cost of the

loan, with the result that the cap effectively sets a maximum limit on the cap holder's borrowing costs.

A cap can be arranged to cover interest periods up to several years in advance.

The main drawback to a cap is the high cost of the premium to purchase it. A lower-cost option is an interest rate collar. A collar is in effect a series of purchased interest rate options and written interest rate put options. A collar can be used to fix a maximum effective borrowing rate, but it also fixes a minimum effective rate.

> **Tutorial note.** Your solution could also have discussed FRAs. However, FRAs are not usually obtainable to cover interest periods in excess of about three years in advance. The effect of an FRA is to fix a future borrowing cost for an interest period. The company would need to arrange a series of FRAs to cover a number of successive interest periods.

28 GROUND PLC

(a) There are three main reasons why a company might enter an interest rate swap transaction.

(i) A company with large borrowings will try to maintain a balance between its fixed rate and its floating rate borrowing. When it suspects that interest rates might be about to rise, it will probably want to have a larger proportion of fixed rate debts. When it expects interest rates to fall, it might want a larger proportion of floating rate loans. Interest rate swaps allow a company to manage the balance between its fixed and floating rate obligations, without having to re-arrange or re-negotiate the underlying loans and bond issues themselves.

(ii) Most fixed rate borrowing is obtained in the bond markets. For many small and medium-sized companies, the bond markets are inaccessible, because bond investors will not buy bonds of companies they consider too great a credit risk. Interest rate swaps assist a company that wants to borrow at a fixed rate, but can only borrow from banks at a floating rate. The company can borrow at a floating rate, and arrange a swap in which it receives a floating rate and pays a fixed rate. This in effect secures fixed rate borrowing for the period of the bank loan.

(iii) Occasionally, an opportunity could arise to benefit from credit arbitrage. Credit arbitrage describes a situation where someone secures a financial benefit from discrepancies in interest rates to borrowers in the financial markets. It might be possible for a company to borrow more cheaply using swaps. For example, a company wishing to borrow at a floating rate of interest might have an opportunity to borrow more cheaply by issuing bonds at a fixed rate and arranging a swap where it receives a fixed rate and pays a floating rate. The net effect will be to pay a floating rate, but a smaller amount than if the company had borrowed directly at a floating rate.

(b) It would appear from the figures that both companies might have an opportunity to benefit from credit arbitrage to borrow more cheaply.

Ground plc wants to borrow at a floating rate. It can do this at LIBOR plus 0.60%. However, it can also borrow at a fixed rate of 7.35% and arrange a swap in which it receives a fixed rate of 7.00% and pays LIBOR.

Ground plc	%
Interest on loan	(7.35)
Swap:	
Receive	7.00
Pay	(LIBOR)
Net interest cost	(LIBOR + 0.35)

The net cost will be LIBOR + 0.35%, which is 0.25% or 25 basis points cheaper than borrowing directly at a floating rate. Ground plc will therefore benefit from a swap.

Putter plc wants to borrow at a fixed rate. It can do this at 8.8%. However, it can also borrow at a floating rate of LIBOR plus 1.35% and arrange a swap in which it pays a fixed rate of 7.25% and receives LIBOR.

Putter plc	%
Interest on loan	(LIBOR + 1.35)
Swap:	
Receive	LIBOR
Pay	(7.25)
Net interest cost	(8.60)

The net cost will be 8.60%, which is 0.20% or 20 basis points cheaper than borrowing directly at a fixed rate. Putter plc will therefore benefit from a swap.

(c) The benefits to Ground plc from using a swap to borrow at a floating rate rather than borrowing directly at a floating rate will be 25 basis points of interest each year for five years.

The value of 25 basis points on a loan of £15 million is 0.0025 × £15 million = £37,500 per year.

Year	*Saving in interest*	*Discount factor a t 9%*	*Present value of savings*
	£		£
1	37,500	0.92	34,500
2	37,500	0.84	31,500
3	37,500	0.77	28,875
4	37,500	0.71	26,625
5	37,500	0.65	24,375
			145,875

Over the period of the swap, LIBOR is higher than it was when the loan and swap were arranged. As a consequence, Ground plc will have to make payments every year to Centre Bank under the swap arrangement. In retrospect, it would have been cheaper for the company to borrow at a fixed rate. However, since it had decided to borrow at a floating rate, using a swap is considerably cheaper in this case than borrowing directly at LIBOR + 60 basis points.

Tutorial note. If you are not sure about the payments, they are set out below. They show how the £37,500 annual saving is derived. These calculations are not necessary for a solution.

Ground could have borrowed at LIBOR plus 60 basis points. Interest rate payments on £15 million would have been:

Year	*LIBOR*	*Borrow at*	*Interest*
	%	%	£
1	7.10	7.70	1,155,000
2 – 5 (per year)	7.80	8.40	1,260,000

Ground borrowed at a fixed rate of 7.35% and interest on this is £1,102,500 each year. The swap payments are as follows.

Year	LIBOR (Ground pays)	Fixed swap rate (Ground receives)	Net payment (Ground pays)	Net payment
y	%	%	%	£
1	7.10	7.00	0.10	15,000
2 – 5 (per year)	7.80	7.00	0.80	120,000

Year	Fixed rate payments	Payments under swap	Total payments	Interest at LIBOR + 60 basis points	Annual saving
	£	£	£	£	£
1	1,102,500	15,000	1,117,500	1,155,000	37,500
2 – 5	1,102,500	120,000	1,222,500	1,260,000	37,500

29 QW PLC

To: Board of Directors, QW plc
From: Treasurer
Date:

(a) **Using financial derivatives and interest rate swaps**

Introduction

The purpose of this report is to explain the nature and function of financial derivatives, and the benefits that they could offer to QW plc. The later sections of the report deal in more detail with methods of hedging interest rate risk, and the potential benefits of negotiating an interest rate swap with ER plc.

Financial derivatives

Financial derivatives are instruments that enable two parties to trade in the price of an underlying financial item, without having to make a transaction in the item itself. Examples of derivative products include futures and options in currencies and interest rates. A future or an option, for example, can be used to trade in the interest rate for an underlying loan or deposit, but without having to obtain a loan or make a deposit.

Financial derivatives can be used to speculate or to hedge exposures to financial risk. For this company, the use of derivatives such as swaps should be to hedge exposures rather than to speculate. If derivatives were used to speculate, the board's concern about the potential risk would be well justified.

Using derivatives to hedge an exposure to risk would benefit the company by reducing its total risk exposure.

Options can be a useful hedging instrument when interest rates or currency exchange rates are volatile, and the direction of future movements in the rate is uncertain. An option provides a hedge against an adverse movement in the rate, but allows the option holder to benefit from any favourable movement in the rate. This is because the option holder can choose not to enforce the transaction.

A forward rate agreement is a forward contract on an interest rate. Whereas a forward exchange contract is a contract to buy and sell currency, an FRA is an agreement on the interest rate for a notional future loan or deposit. Although it is a forward interest rate contract, it is also a form of derivative. If FRAs are classed as derivatives, it is impossible to hedge an exposure to future interest rate changes without using derivatives.

An advantage of swaps is that they can sometimes enable a company to borrow more cheaply, due to differences in interest rate in the market. Making use of available interest rates and a swap to reduce net borrowing costs is known as credit arbitrage.

However, derivatives have some disadvantages, and should be used carefully by non-bank companies.

(i) Currency derivatives are more complex than simple forward exchange contracts. They are also much less widely used than forward exchange contracts.

(ii) The cost of buying options (option premiums) can be high.

(iii) Interest rate exposure for many companies is not particularly significant, and such companies have no requirement for interest rate derivatives.

(b) **Features and advantages of swaps compared with other derivatives**

An interest rate coupon swap is an arrangement whereby two companies, or a company and a bank, swap interest rate commitments with each other, usually for a period of several years. One party pays a fixed rate of interest on a notional amount of principal, and the other party pays a variable rate, usually LIBOR in the case of sterling swaps. The exchange of interest payments can be timed to correspond with interest payment commitments on an underlying debt, such as a bank loan or a bond issue.

The main purposes of a coupon swap are:

(i) To change a company's interest payments from fixed rate to floating rate or vice versa.

(ii) To enable a company to take on fixed interest rate commitments when it can only borrow in the 'cash market' at a variable rate.

(iii) On occasion, to reduce interest costs, through credit arbitrage.

The main advantages of swaps over other interest rate derivatives is that:

(i) They are long-term instruments, and can be arranged for the full period of a loan.

(ii) Transaction costs are quite low, and they can easily be reversed.

(iii) They can be used to reduce net borrowing costs. Companies with different credit ratings can borrow at the best cost in the market that is most accessible to them and then swap this benefit with another company to reduce the mutual borrowing costs.

(iv) Swaps allow capital restructuring by changing the nature of interest commitments without the need to redeem debt or to issue new debt, thus reducing transaction costs.

(c) **Implications of an interest rate swap with ER plc**

The proposed swap would involve one company borrowing at a floating rate, and the other at a fixed rate. Each company would enter into an individual loan arrangement with the bank, and the interest rate liabilities would then be swapped.

	Fixed	*Floating*
	%	%
QW can borrow at	8.00	LIBOR + 0.20
ER can borrow at	9.50	LIBOR + 0.90
Difference	1.50	0.70

QW wants to borrow at a floating rate but can borrow relatively more cheaply at a fixed rate than ER. ER wants to borrow at a fixed rate but can borrow relatively more cheaply at a floating rate than QW.

There is scope for credit arbitrage of (1.50 – 0.70)% = 0.80%. If the arranging bank takes commission of 0.20%, this leaves a 'profit' from arranging a swap of 0.60%.

The net result should therefore be that:

1 by arranging a swap with the bank, QW should end up with net borrowing costs of LIBOR minus 0.10% (0.30% less than borrowing directly at a floating rate).

2 by arranging a swap with the bank, ER should end up with net borrowing costs of 9.20% (0.30% less than borrowing directly at a floating rate).

QW

	%
Borrow at fixed rate, pay	(8.00)
Swap	
Pay floating rate	(LIBOR)
Receive fixed rate (balancing figure)	8.10
Net borrowing cost	(LIBOR – 0.10)

ER

	%
Borrow at floating rate, pay	(LIBOR + 0.90)
Swap	
Receive floating rate	LIBOR
Pay fixed rate (balancing figure)	(8.30)
Net borrowing cost	(9.20)

The bank's commission comes from the difference between the fixed rate it receives from ER (8.30%) and the fixed rate it pays to QW (8.10%).

The saving of 0.30% interest on £10 million will reduce the net borrowing cost of each company by £30,000 each year for the three-year term of their loans.

30 ARK PLC

(a) If interest rates remain at their current levels, the interest payable in the six months under review will be as follows.

Amount of borrowing	£12m
Interest rate (base + 1.5%)	7.5% pa
Period of borrowing	3 months
Interest (£12m × 7.5% × 3/12)	£225,000

> **Tutorial note.** The requirement of the treasury team is that interest charges should not exceed £235,000 (£225,000 + £10,000). Any interest rate hedge will therefore be based on the assumption that interest rates will rise.

(b) **Hedge using futures**

Either March or June contracts could be used. Since the actual loan will be taken out around 1 March, March contracts will be used.

The number of futures contracts required is (£12 million/ £500,000 per contract) = 24 contracts. Since the company wants to hedge against a fall in interest rates, it will sell futures.

The value of each movement in the futures price of 0.01 is:

£500,000 × 0.01% × 3/12 = £12.50.

A movement of 1.8% in the futures price equates to 180 ticks. Since interest rates have risen, the futures price will fall from 93.45 to 91.65.

The procedure the company would follow is as below.

1 December: Sell March futures at 93.45
To close the position: Buy futures at 91.65.

The profit on the transaction would be:
24 contracts × 180 ticks × £12.50 = £54,000.

Interest payable on the three-month loan will be 9.5%, because rates have risen by 2%. Interest payable will therefore be £12 million × 9.5% × 3/12 = £285,000

The profit on the futures trading of £54,000 can be offset against the cost of the 2% rise in interest rates.

The net interest is therefore: £285,000 – £54,000 = £231,000.
This is within the maximum cost limit that the treasury team has set.

(c) **Hedge using options on futures**

The company wants to hedge against the risk of a rise in interest rates. Using futures, it would sell futures to create this hedge. Using options on futures, it will therefore need the option to sell futures. This is achieved by purchasing put options.

Put options with an exercise price of 93.50 are purchased. Since 24 futures contracts would be needed for a hedge, the company would sell 24 options on March futures.

The procedure is as follows.

1 December: Buy 24 puts on March futures at a strike price of 93.50. Premium cost = 1.25

1 March: The futures price has fallen by 1.80, from its 1 December value of 93.45 to 91.65.

1 March: Exercise right to sell March futures at 93.50

Buy March futures at 91.65

The profit on the futures trading, after deducting the cost of the option premium, is:

93.50 – 91.65 – 1.25 = 60 ticks.

The total profit on the options and futures trading (24 contracts, with a value of £12.50 per tick of price)

= 60 ticks × £12.50 per tick × 24 contracts = £18,000.

As calculated above, the total actual interest cost of borrowing at 9.5% for three months is £285,000.

The profit on the futures trading of £18,000 can be offset against the cost of the 2% rise in interest rates.

The net interest is therefore: £285,000 – £18,000 = £267,000.

This is above the maximum cost limit that the treasury team has set.

The problem of using options on futures in this case has been the cost of the option premiums.

(d) Alternative derivative products that could be considered include the following.

(i) **A forward rate agreement (FRA).** An FRA is an agreement with a bank to fix the rate of interest on a notional principal amount, for an interest period starting at some time in the future. In this example, the company could buy an FRA giving it the right to borrow £12 million for three months in three months' time (a 3 v 6 FRA) at a rate of interest that is fixed in the FRA agreement. If the interest rate (LIBOR) rises above the FRA rate, the bank will compensate the company for the difference. However, if the interest rate fell below the FRA rate, the company would have to make a compensation payment to the bank. An FRA has the net effect of fixing the future interest rate the company will have to pay on its future borrowing.

(ii) Over the counter (OTC) interest rate options (also known as interest rate guarantees) are similar to the traded options on interest rate futures. However, instead of being purchased on a futures exchange, they are obtained from a bank and tailored to suit the company's specific requirements. The company would also be able to arrange some form of collar to minimise the premium cost. It could negotiate to buy a borrower's option at one strike rate and sell a lender's option to the bank at a lower strike rate. This would effectively fix the borrowing cost between the two rates, but the premium cost would be the difference between the purchase cost of the borrower's option and the revenue from the sale of the lender's option.

31 SLICE COMMUNICATIONS

(a) The maximum cost that Slice Communications plc wants to pay for its borrowing £18 million for 3 months is 7.5%. The interest cost of borrowing at this rate would be: £18m × 3/12 × 7.5% = £337,500.

(i) **Hedging the borrowing rate using futures**

The start date of borrowing is in two months on 1 February 20X1, so March or June contracts can be used. Since March is the nearer date, March contracts will be chosen.

The company can hedge its exposure to the risk of a rise in interest rates by selling futures. Selling futures now will mean a profit will be made if interest rates rise and the futures are bought back at a lower price. £18m/£0.5m = 36 contracts will be needed. Sell 36 contracts at 93.10.

The tick value of the contract is 0.01% × 500,000 × 3/12 = £12.50.

The price of the March future is for an interest rate of (100 – 93.10) 6.90%. If LIBOR rises by 150 basis points to 8%, the question states that the price of the March future would rise by 130 basis points. This would be from 6.90% to 8.20%, and the price of the future on 1 February would be (100 – 8.20) = 91.80. The company will borrow £18 million for three months at (8% + 0.75%) 8.75%. It will also buy 36 futures at 91.80, to close its futures position.

The results of the hedge are shown below.

		£
Interest cost on loan at 8.75%	(£18 million × 3/12 × 8.75%)	393,750
Futures		
Sell at 93.10		
Buy at 91.80		
Gain per contract:	130 ticks	
Total gain (36 contracts)	130 × 36 × £12.50	58,500
Net cost		335,250

This is within the cost limit the company set for the borrowing.

(ii) **Hedging the borrowing rate using traded options**

The start date of borrowing is in two months on 1 February 20X1, so March or June contracts can be used. March options will be used, for the same reason that March futures would be used with a futures hedge.

The company needs options to sell futures. It should therefore buy put options at 93.50.

Buying put options will mean a profit will be made if interest rates rise and the holder has the right to sell interest rate futures contracts at a higher price than their market value at close out.

£18m/£0.5m = 36 contracts will be needed.

The options are priced in % per annum, ie ticks. The tick value is £12.50.

The option premium will be 36 × 12.50 × 60 ticks = £27,000.

If the futures price is 91.80 on 1 February, the company will exercise its options to sell futures at 93.50, and it will buy options at 91.80 to close its position. It will borrow for three months at the current rate of (8% + 0.75%) 8.75%.

The results of the hedge are shown below.

		£
Interest cost on loan at 8.75%	(£18 million × 3/12 × 8.75%)	393,750
Cost of options (premiums)		27,000
Futures		
Sell at 93.50		
Buy at 91.80		
Gain per contract:	170 ticks	
Total gain (36 contracts)	170 × 36 × £12.50	(76,500)
Net cost		344,250

This is over the cost limit the company set for the borrowing.

Options are a more expensive hedging method when the interest rate goes up, because of the cost of the premiums. However, if interest rates had gone down, not up, options would be a cheaper hedging method than futures. This is because options allow the company to benefit from a fall in the interest rate, since the options would not be exercised and the company could borrow at the (lower) market rate of interest. With futures, the company is effectively locking itself into an interest rate for the borrowing.

(b) The advantages of exchange-traded interest rate options are as follows.

(i) The prices are clearly visible and no negotiation on price is required.
(ii) The market place gives quick access to buyers and sellers.
(iii) The options can be sold if not required, at any time to expiry.
(iv) Gains or losses are computed ('marked to market') on a daily basis.
(v) Traded options are normally American-style (ie they can be exercised at any time). They are more flexible than many OTC options, which are European-style (ie can only be exercised at the maturity date).

The main advantage of OTC options is that they can be tailored more exactly to the needs of the purchaser, in terms of maturity date, contract size, currency and nature of interest. Contract sizes are larger than on the traded markets and longer times to expiry are available.

(c) Interest rate option prices are affected by the following factors.

(i) The price of the specific interest-bearing security which the option gives the right to buy or sell (eg a notional deposit at the LIBOR interest rate), compared with the exercise price for the option. In-the-money options will cost more than out-of-the-money options.

(ii) The remaining time to expiry of the option. The premium varies with time to expiry, and longer-dated options will cost more.

(iii) The volatility in the price of the underlying item. The premium will be higher when the price of the underlying item is more volatile, and subject to large changes up or down in the remaining time to expiry.

(iv) The current interest rate also has some effect on the premium for an option.

Options can seem expensive, but this is because they act like an insurance policy, providing protection against increased interest costs but allowing the purchaser to take advantage of interest rate falls. OTC option prices are not as transparent as market traded options, but there is a competitive market of banks and other sellers. As a safeguard, prices can be checked against option pricing models and inexperienced purchasers are advised to seek advice in this respect.

32 FUTURES AND OPTIONS

(a) REPORT

To: Board of Directors
From:
Date:

Subject: Use of financial futures by the company

The purpose of this report is to deal with three main areas: the benefits of financial futures; the risks of using futures; and strategies for the minimisation of futures risks.

The benefits of futures

Futures are a form of exchange-traded forward contract, which give a fixed rate for a financial instrument, such as security prices, exchange rates or interest rates, at a future date. Financial futures can be used to hedge against risks of movements in:

(i) government bond prices (eg gilts prices)
(ii) short-term interest rates
(iii) foreign currency exchange rates, and
(iv) share prices

For a manufacturing company, the principal advantage of futures is likely to be the hedging of interest rates, and possibly share prices where the company holds an equity portfolio. Forward exchange contracts are readily available for the reduction of exchange rate exposure, and are likely to be a better hedging method than currency futures.

A company with a large amount of variable rate borrowings could be concerned about a possible rise in the level of interest rates. It could sell interest rate futures, so that if interest rates rise, its borrowing costs will also rise, but the higher borrowing costs will be offset by profits on futures trading. The same type and amount of futures contracts that have been sold may be bought at a cheaper price, to close out the futures position, and the profit made on the futures deals will compensate for any extra loan interest that the company must pay.

The risks of futures

Futures hedges are unlikely to be perfect, for the following reasons.

(i) The movement in futures prices may not be an exact reflection of the movement in interest rates.

(ii) Futures contracts are of a standard size, and it may not be possible to match exactly the amount of the borrowings.

(iii) A company might not know exactly what its interest rate exposures are, and so arranging a hedge will inevitably be inexact. When a company has arranged a hedge, but the underlying exposure does not exist, the 'hedge' will become a speculative position.

(iv) A company's treasury department might be tempted to use financial futures for speculation, to improve the 'profit' of the treasury department. If speculation by the treasury department is to be permitted, it should be controlled. For example, limits should be placed on the size of speculative positions allowed.

Strategies for the minimisation of futures risk

Internal rules should be formulated to allow the use of futures to hedge against known specific financial risks, but to restrict the use of futures in open speculation. Principles to be used include the following.

(i) There should be strict limits on the size of contracts that may be used.

(ii) The responsibility for reporting on futures activity should be separate from the responsibility for decision making on futures trading.

(iii) The use of derivatives should be centralised, with local management not being allowed to trade in derivatives.

(iv) Futures activity should be subject to regular detailed scrutiny by an independent department such as internal or external audit, reporting to the audit committee.

(b) Collars make use of interest rate options to limit exposure to the risk of movement in rates. The company wants to set a minimum yield on its cash deposits, and could do this either by purchasing over-the-counter put options or by purchasing call options on interest rate futures. However, the cost of the premium could be high. A collar is an alternative arrangement: this sets a minimum interest yield, but also a maximum yield. With a collar, a company is therefore arranging both a cap (an upper limit) and a floor (a lower limit) on its interest yield.

A collar can be created either by purchasing over-the-counter interest rate put options (lenders' options) and selling call options (borrowers' options). Alternatively it can purchase call options on interest rate futures (to set a minimum interest yield) and sell put options on futures (which will set maximum limit on the interest yield).

The use of the cap means that the cost is lower than for a floor alone, because the cost of the call options is offset to some extent by the income from selling the put options.

Since the company requires protection for the next eight months, it will need to use March options in order to cover the full period. Let's assume that the floor will be fixed at the current yield of 7.5%. This implies that it will buy call options at 9250.

At the same time, the company will limit its ability to benefit from rises in rates by selling put options at a higher rate, say at 8.0% (or 9200).

If the company does take out the options as described above, the effect will be as follows.

(i) If interest rates fall below 7.5%, it will exercise the call options and effectively fix its interest rate at 7.5%. The loss on the interest rate movement will be borne by the seller of the call option.

(ii) If interest rates remain between the 7.5% floor and the 8.0% ceiling, neither the call options nor the put options will be exercised. The company will benefit from any increase in rates above 7.5% within this band, to the extent that it will earn a higher interest yield on its cash deposits.

(iii) If interest rates rise above 8.0%, the buyer of the put options will exercise the options once the futures price falls below 9200. The company will effectively achieve an interest rate of 8.0%, but the benefit of any increase in the interest rate above 8.0% will accrue to the buyer of the put options.

The company has deposits of £9.75 million. To hedge the interest rate exposure with options on futures, it would need to buy (£9.75 m/£500,000 per contract) = 19.5, say 20 call option contracts at 92.50 and sell the same number of put options at 92.00. The call options will cost 68 and the put options will sell for 13. The net cost of the collar is therefore 55 per pair of contracts.

The total cost of the options hedge is therefore 20 contracts × 55 ticks × £12.50 per tick = £13,750.

33 OPTIONS AND SWAPS

(a) It appears that although interest rates are likely to rise over the next five months, it is possible that they could fall instead. In this type of situation, options are useful in that they allow the company to be protected against adverse rate movements but at the same time to benefit if the rate does move in the company's favour. The drawback to the use of interest rate options is that the premium costs tend to be quite high. However, the company could restrict the premium costs by using a collar.

If the company did not use options, but simply borrowed the money at LIBOR + 1.5%, the extreme outcomes are as follows.

Interest rates rise by 1%

The additional cost incurred would be £5m × 1% × 3/12 = £12,500.

Interest rates fall by 0.75%

The saving in cost would be £5m × 0.75% × 3/12 = £9,375.

If the company used options for the three-month period, it would need the following number of contracts, the contract size being £0.5m, and the contract period being three months:

(£5m ÷ £0.5m) = 10 contracts.

If the company used interest rate futures to hedge the risk of an increase in interest rates, it would sell futures. Using options on futures, it should buy the right to sell futures, therefore it must purchase June put options.

Since LIBOR is currently at 7%, the company might select contracts with an exercise price of 93.00 (100.00 – 7.00) to protect itself fully against rate increases.

The outcomes of this course of action would be as follows.

Interest rates rise by 1%

If interest rates rise by 1%, the June futures price would fall by 1% from 92.50 to 91.50. Since this is below the option price of 93.00, the option would be exercised, giving a profit of 150 ticks. The profit on the contract would therefore be:

		£
Profit arising on the contract	10 × 150 × £12.50	18,750
Less premium cost	10 × 59 × £12.50	(7,375)
		11,375

The profit on the contract is less than the additional interest costs incurred of £12,500 as calculated above. There is therefore a net loss of £1,125 (£12,500 – £11,375).

Interest rates fall by 0.75%

If interest rates fall, then the option would not be exercised. The company would benefit from the drop in rates calculated above, but it would still incur the premium on the option contracts. Compared with a policy of hedging the interest rate exposure now with financial futures, there is a net profit of £2,000 (£9,375 – £7,375).

The company can alternatively reduce the option premium cost by using a collar.

(b) (i) Compare the rates at which the two companies can borrow from the market:

	Fixed	*Floating*
Our company	8.35%	LIBOR + 0.60%
Bravo plc	10.80%	LIBOR + 1.35%
Differential	2.45%	0.75%

	%
Difference between the differentials (1.45% - 0.75%)	1.70
Less: bank commission for arranging the swap	0.25
Available for arbitrage gain	1.45
Gain required by our company	0.30
Gain available for Bravo plc	1.15

Our company has comparative advantage borrowing fixed rate, so it will gain if it borrows at a fixed rate and swaps into floating rate. The reverse is true for Bravo plc. The arbitrage gain figures show that a swap can be arranged which will benefit all parties, with the gain for Bravo being very large indeed.

(ii) Amount borrowed = £15m.

If we borrow at fixed rate of 8.35%, the annual interest will be £1,252,500.

We will benefit by 30 basis points from the swap, which means that the net borrowing cost will be LIBOR plus (60 – 30) basis points, ie LIBOR plus 30 bp.

If we pay LIBOR in the swap, we will need to receive (8.35% - 0.30%) = 8.05% fixed in the swap.

1 For the first year, LIBOR is 8.5%. The cash flows will be:

	£	£
Pay interest on fixed rate loan		(1,252,500)
Swap		
Received fixed interest (8.05% of £15m)	1,207,500	
Pay LIBOR (8.5% of £15m)	(1,275,000)	
Net swap payment		(67,500)
Total interest cost		(1,320,000)

The effective interest rate is therefore (£1,320,000/£15m) = 8.80%, which is 30 basis points above the LIBOR rate for the period.

2 For the following years, LIBOR is 10%. The cash flows will be:

	£	£
Pay interest on fixed rate loan		(1,252,500)
Swap		
Receive fixed interest (8.05% of £15m)	1,207,500	
Pay LIBOR (10% of £15m)	(1,500,000)	
Net swap payment		(292,500)
Total interest cost		(1,545,000)

The effective interest rate is therefore (£1,545,000/£15m) = 10.30%, which is 30 basis points above the LIBOR rate for the period.

In retrospect, it is clear that the company could have borrowed more cheaply by sticking to the fixed rate of 8.35%. However, the decision was to borrow at a floating rate, and the swap has allowed the company to borrow at LIBOR plus 30 basis points, an annual saving of 30 basis points (£45,000 on a loan of £15 million) compared with borrowing directly at LIBOR plus 60 bp.

34 CORPORATE GOVERNANCE

(a) Corporate governance can be defined broadly as the system by which an organisation is directed and controlled. It is concerned with systems, processes, controls, accountability and decision making at the heart of and at the highest level of an organisation. It is therefore concerned with the way in which top managers execute their responsibilities and authority and how they account for that authority to those who have entrusted them with assets and resources. In particular it is concerned with the potential abuse of power and the need for openness, integrity and accountability in corporate decision making.

A key issue in corporate governance is the problem that major public companies are run by powerful executives, who do not necessarily manage the company in the best interests of its owners, the shareholders.

In principle, the shareholders appoint a board of directors and an external auditor and need to satisfy themselves that an appropriate governance structure exists. The board of directors is responsible for running the company on behalf of shareholders, considering the interests of other stakeholders such as employees, and reporting to shareholders on the company's progress. The auditor provides an independent examination of the company's financial statements. In practice, there is widespread concern that executives run a company more for their own benefit than for the benefit of the shareholders, and that the role of external auditors is not a sufficient check.

Clearly, a company must have senior executives. The problem is how to ensure as far as possible that the actions and decisions of the executives will be for the benefit of shareholders. Measures that have been adopted in the UK have been as follows.

(i) A listed company is required by the 'voluntary' Combined Code to appoint non-executive directors. The non-executives are intended to provide a check or balance against the power of the chairman and chief executive.

(ii) The Combined Code recommends that the posts of chairman and chief executive should not be held by the same person, to prevent excessive executive power being held by one individual.

(iii) The Combined Code also recommends that non-executive directors should make up the membership of the remuneration committee of the board, and should determine the remuneration of executive directors. This is partly to prevent the executives deciding their own pay, and rewarding themselves excessively.

Another purpose is to try to devise incentive schemes for executives that will motivate them to achieve results for the company that will also be in the best interests of the shareholders.

The Combined Code requirement for a risk audit should ensure that the board of directors is aware of the risks facing the company, and have systems in place for managing them. In theory, this should provide some protection against risk for the company's shareholders.

The Combined Code encourages greater dialogue between a company and its shareholders. Institutional investor organisations such as the ABI are also encouraging greater participation by shareholders, for example in voting.

The audit committee of the board is seen as having a major role to play, in promoting dialogue between the external auditors and the board. Corporate governance should be improved if the views of the external auditors are given greater consideration.

(b) The relationship between management and shareholders is sometimes referred to as an agency relationship, in which managers act as agents for the shareholders, using delegated powers to run the affairs of the company in the shareholders' best interests. There is a potential conflict of interest that is inherent in this situation, since shareholders will be best rewarded by efficient performance, while managers may prefer a life where they don't have to work too intensively and in which they are rewarded by high salaries and perks. Other interest groups such as employees, suppliers, customers and the government may also have objectives that conflict with those of the shareholders.

Goal congruence occurs when the goals of the different interest groups coincide with those of the company as a whole. There have been many attempts to change the way in which managers are remunerated so as to improve the achievement of goal congruence between the managers and the shareholders, and the provision of share options form one of these methods.

In a share option scheme, selected employees can be given a number of share options, each of which gives the holder the right after a certain date to subscribe for shares in the company at a fixed price. The value of an option will increase if the company is successful and its share price goes up. The theory is that this will encourage managers to pursue high NPV strategies and investments, since they as shareholders will benefit personally from the increase in the share price that results from such investments.

However, although share option schemes can contribute to the achievement of goal congruence, there are a number of reasons why the benefits may not be as great as might be expected, as follows.

(i) Managers are protected from the downside risk that is faced by shareholders. If the share price falls, they do not have to take up the shares and will still receive their standard remuneration, while shareholders will lose money.

(ii) Many other factors as well as the quality of the company's performance influence share price movements. If the market is rising strongly, managers will still benefit from share options, even if performance has been worse than expected. Similarly, even though the company may have been very successful, the share price will fall if there is a downward stock market adjustment, and the managers will not be rewarded for their efforts in the way that was planned.

(iii) The scheme may encourage management to adopt 'creative accounting' methods that will distort the reported performance of the company in the service of the managers' own ends.

(iv) There have been reported instances where executives have persuaded the remuneration committee to amend the share option scheme when the share price has fallen sharply (so that the options are out-of-the-money or 'under water'), and issue new options at a lower exercise price. Unlike shareholders, executives are therefore protected against the share price fall with this type of arrangement.

35 OECD

(a) Corporate governance is a set of relationships between a company's shareholders, its board, its management and other stakeholders. The OECD states that a major reason for encouraging better corporate governance is to improve economic efficiency. A system of corporate governance provides a structure for setting the corporate objectives of the organisation, and for achieving those objectives, and for monitoring performance along the way. Better corporate governance will result in a greater probability of clear objectives being set and achieved. A greater probability of success in achieving objectives should arise by:

(i) providing incentives for the board and management to pursue objectives that are in the interests of the company and its shareholders, and

(ii) facilitating effective monitoring, to ensure that resources are used more efficiently.

The main concern of the OECD principles is with issues arising from the separation of ownership of a company (by the shareholders) from control (by the board of directors and management).

Where corporate governance is weak, it will act as a deterrent to inward investment by investors who are based in a country (such as the US) where standards of corporate governance are higher.

(b) The key participants in a system of corporate governance are as follows.

(i) The board of directors. In a continental-style two-tier board system, this is the supervisory board.

(ii) The senior management. In a continental-style two-tier board system, this is the management board.

(iii) The controlling shareholders, if there are any.

(iv) Institutional investors, who demand more influence (and in the UK who might follow the corporate governance guidelines issued by their industry body, such as the ABI or NAPF).

(v) Small shareholders, who should expect fair treatment from management and any controlling shareholder, particularly in matters such as takeover bids.

(vi) Creditors, who act as an external monitor over company performance. This is particularly the case with major creditors such as bondholders.

(vii) Employees, who contribute to the long-term success of the company.

(viii) The government, especially if it has a conscious wish to create an institutional and legal framework for a satisfactory system of corporate governance.

(c) The OECD principles are grouped into five broad areas.

(i) One area deals with the rights of shareholders, and the need for companies to ensure that shareholders' rights are protected. Shareholders should not have the right to take over the running of their company, but they should have rights as shareholders, such as the right to a secure method of registering the ownership of their shares, a right to vote at company general meetings, a right to elect the directors, a right to regular information about the company's performance, a right to share in the profits of the company and a right to transfer their shares. They should also be allowed to participate in decisions that will affect the company in a fundamental way, such as changes to the constitution (articles of association) and authorising the issue of new shares. A concern of the OECD has been that overseas investors are not always granted these rights, particularly in matters of voting at general meetings.

(ii) A second area of OECD principles is concerned with the equitable treatment of shareholders. Shareholders should have a means of obtaining effective redress for the violation of their rights, and the effectiveness of the country's legal system or regulatory system is an important element in this. Within any class of shares, all shareholders should have the same rights, and the OECD urges strong regulation against insider dealing (or market abuse).

(iii) A third area of OECD principles is concerned with the role of stakeholders in corporate governance. The OECD states that the success of a company results from teamwork that embodies the contributions of a range of different resource providers, including investors, employees, creditors and suppliers. The principles include the requirement for companies to ensure that respect is given to the rights of stakeholders that are protected by law (eg employment law, contract law and insolvency law). A further principle is that there should be 'employment-enhancing mechanisms for stakeholder participation', such as employee share ownership schemes or profit-sharing schemes.

(iv) A fourth area of OECD principles is concerned with disclosure and transparency. There should be timely and accurate disclosure of information on all material matters affecting the company, such as its financial situation and performance, and corporate governance. The OECD also suggests that information about risk should be provided. Information produced by a company should be audited, and the annual audit should be carried out by an independent auditor.

(v) The fifth area of principles deals with the responsibilities of the board of directors. The board should fulfil certain key functions, which are listed in the principles. They include reviewing and guiding corporate strategy, risk policy, setting the annual budget and performance objectives. The board is also responsible for ensuring the effectiveness of corporate governance, and should be capable of exercising independent judgement on the company's affairs.

(d) It is unusual for major global companies to have two or more classes of equity shares, but such cases do exist. The OECD principles do not state that such arrangements should not be allowed. The principles do state, however, that where the capital structure allows certain shareholders to obtain a degree of control that is disproportionate to the size of their shareholding, there should be a full disclosure. Any other investor in the company's shares will therefore have full warning.

36 NON-EXECUTIVES

(a) A non-executive director is a director on the board of a company who does not have any executive responsibilities. A NED is not independent if he or she is on the board representing the interests of a major shareholder, because the views given by the director will be made in the interests of that shareholder. Similarly, it is debatable whether a director is independent when he or she has a close relationship with the company or any other executive director. For example, for a former chief executive of a company might be given a non-executive role after retirement. He would not be independent. In contrast, an independent NED is a person who has no other connection with the company other than as non-executive director, and who should be able to give an independent opinion on the affairs of the company, without influence from any other director or any shareholder.

(b) A potential conflict of interests occurs when the executive directors or senior management of a company might be inclined to take decisions that would not be in the interests of the company's shareholders. Although there are several areas where a conflict of interest could arise, the major problem areas are those of remuneration of the directors and senior managers, financial reporting, and nominations of new board members.

If executive directors are allowed to decide their own remuneration, they could be inclined to pay themselves as much as possible, without having to hold themselves to account or to justify their high pay. Where incentive schemes are in place, there is a risk that incentive schemes devised by the executive directors for themselves will be linked to achieving performance targets that are not necessarily in the shareholders' interests. For example, rewarding directors with a bonus for achieving profit growth is of no value to shareholders if the result is higher business risk and a lower share price. In the UK, the Combined Code calls for a remuneration committee of the board to be established to decide on directors' pay, including incentive schemes, and for this committee to be filled by NEDs. The NEDs should, in principle, be able to devise fair remuneration packages that include an incentive element, in which the performance targets bring the objectives of the executive directors more into line with those of the shareholders.

A second potential area for conflict of interest is financial reporting. The executive directors might be tempted to 'window dress' the results of the company, in order to present the financial results in a way that reflects better on themselves and their achievements. It is therefore suggested that there should be an audit committee of the board, consisting of non-executive directors, whose task should be to consider issues relating to financial reporting and financial control systems. This committee should be responsible for maintaining regular liaison with the external auditors.

A third potential area for conflict is nominations of new board members. A powerful chairman or chief executive could be tempted to appoint their supporters or 'yes men' to the board, and so strengthen their position on the board. The Combined Code recommends that there should be a nominations committee of the board, manned by NEDs.

Other areas of potential conflict of interest can be identified, such as succession planning, and the board's decisions on making acquisitions or in preparing defences against a takeover bid. In each of these areas, NEDs should be able to provide a counter-balance to the self-interested views of executive directors.

(c) The system of NEDs is criticised for the weaknesses stated in the question. Any director should have sufficient time to perform his or her duties effectively. The position of director carries a large amount of responsibility, and when a person who is an NED of one company is an executive director of another, most of his time will presumably be devoted to his executive responsibilities. It could be argued that senior executives should have time to act as NED on the board of one or two other public companies. It is much more difficult to argue, however, that a person can operate effectively as an NED on the boards of five or more companies, as well as holding down an executive position. When an NED does not have the time to do a proper job, it will bring the entire system of NEDs into disrepute.

A second major objection to the system of NEDs is that when a large number of NEDs are executive directors of other companies, they have an interest in not causing trouble or asking difficult questions. If an NED creates problems for the executive directors of the companies where he is an NED, there is every likelihood that his own NEDs will cause a similar problem for him in the company where he is an executive director. When senior executives are appointed to each other's boards, there is a view that this creates a 'club' of individuals with common interests. For example, if NEDs sit on the remuneration committee and award high pay packages to the executives, they can expect their own NEDs in turn to award high levels of remuneration to them.

(d) In the UK, it is still the norm for NEDs to receive a fixed cash payment for their services, without any incentives. However, some companies pay their NEDs in shares. They would argue that the more equity the NEDs hold, the more likely they will be to look at issues from the point of view of the shareholders. There is a risk that an NED holding shares could become more concerned with short-term movements in the share price and the opportunity of making a short-term profit from selling their shares. However, a suitable precaution against this could be to obtain the agreement of a NED not to sell his or her shares until after leaving the board.

The argument that NEDs should be rewarded with share options is more contentious, but it is widely practised in the UK and is even more common in the US. The argument against rewarding NEDs with share options is that this form of remuneration could align the interests of the NEDs more closely with the executive directors, who also hold share options. NEDs should give independent advice, and it can be argued that it is therefore not appropriate to incentivise them in the same way as the executives.

A further argument is that when executive directors are rewarded with share options, it is up to the NEDs on the remuneration committee to set the targets that must be reached before the options are exercised. Being part of a similar share option scheme could compromise their judgement. (*Tutorial note*: This view has been expressed by the head of investment of the ABI, and reported in the Financial Times, 31 October 2001).

It would appear that in the UK, institutional investors would prefer NEDs to be rewarded with cash or shares rather than share options.

37 AUDIT AND GOVERNANCE

(a) The role of the external auditors pre-dates formal systems of corporate governance. By law, the external auditors are required to make a statement in the annual accounts as to whether the accounts give a true and fair view of the state of affairs of the company as at the balance sheet date and of its profit for the period covered by the accounts.

In the UK, one of the factors giving rise to the pressure for better corporate governance was concern that some large companies were not providing fair accounts, and that profits or asset values were, in some cases, artificially inflated. There was a view that the external auditors were unable to perform their function properly, perhaps because a powerful or unscrupulous chief executive could keep information away from them.

There have also been criticisms that the external auditors of a company are not always as independent as they should be, because they rely on the company not just for their audit fee, but for substantial fees for other consultancy work throughout the year.

Under the UK's Combined Code on corporate governance, large public companies are expected to have an audit committee of the board of directors, consisting of non-executive directors. One of the functions of the audit committee should be to maintain an appropriate relationship with the auditors, which means that the views of the auditors should be heard by the NEDs. The committee should also establish formal arrangements for considering how they should apply the principles for financial reporting and internal control, and the requirement to liase with the external auditors means that the opinions of the auditors on financial reporting and internal controls will be fed into this process.

Interestingly, another function of the audit committee should be to keep under review the independence and objectivity of the external auditors, particularly where they perform a large amount of non-audit services for the company.

(b) Internal controls are rules and procedures that are put in place to ensure that operations are carried out properly, efficiently and effectively, that the company's assets are safeguarded, that the company's internal and external reporting systems are reliable and that relevant laws and regulations are complied with.

Many internal controls are financial controls, such as procedures to ensure that proper accounting records are kept, that financial information produced by the company is reliable, that the company is not unnecessarily exposed to financial risks, that assets are safeguarded and that fraud is prevented or detected when it occurs.

The Turnbull report recommended that listed companies are expected to have in place a robust system of internal control, which should be reviewed at least annually. The features of a sound system of controls are that:

(i) it should facilitate the efficient and effective operation of the company, by enabling it to respond to the risks that it faces

(ii) help to ensure the quality of internal and external reporting, and

(iii) help to ensure compliance with relevant laws and regulations.

Regular internal control reports to the board should consider the significant risks facing the company, the effectiveness of existing controls for managing them and whether any further measures are needed to remedy control weaknesses.

(c) An internal audit department would be responsible for monitoring the internal controls within the company, and for checking that they are adequate and functioning properly. The department might also be required to recommend improvements in the control system where there appear to be weaknesses.

The Turnbull report states that the need for an internal audit department will depend on various factors, such as the scale, diversity and complexity of the company's operations, and on the number of employees. However, in the absence of an internal audit function, management must have other monitoring processes in place to ensure that the system of controls is functioning. The report also states that a company without an internal audit function should each year review the need for one.

The Listing Rules also include a requirement that if a company does not have an internal audit department and has not reviewed the need for one during the year, it should disclose this fact in the annual report and accounts.

(d) The requirement that the positions of chief executive and chairman should not be held by the same person is to prevent too much power within a company falling into the hands of one individual. The Combined Code states that there should be a clear division at the head of the company, to ensure a balance of power and authority, and to prevent any one individual having unfettered power over decision-making.

Any decision by a company to combine the roles of chairman and chief executive should be publicly justified.

38 REMUNERATION

(a) Measures for monitoring performance of a company, and individuals, can be grouped into three categories, market-based measures, earnings-based measures and internal performance measures.

(i) Market-based measures of performance are based on the movement in the market price of the company's shares over a given time period. An advantage of this method of performance measure is that it is aligned closely to the creation of shareholder value, which is generally assumed to be the prime objective of a company. A drawback to market-based measures is that share price movements fluctuate continually with supply and demand, and the prices that are used to measure the rise or fall in the share price over a period might not be properly representative of their true market worth.

A widely-used market-based measure is Total Shareholder Return (TSR) which is a measure of the return earned by shareholders over a given period, in terms of dividends received and movements in the share price. The return is expressed as a percentage of the share price at the start of the period.

A limitation of market-based measures is that although they can measure company performance, they cannot identify which individuals contributed to the achievement of the return. Nevertheless, a market-based return measure could be used as a basis for the incentive remuneration scheme for a chief executive.

(ii) Earnings-based measures of performance are based on profit-related measures of performance, such as EPS, growth in EPS and return on investment. Although widely-used in incentive packages, earnings-based measures have several weaknesses. They are short-term measures of profit, and ignore the longer term, ie what an individual has achieved that will affect future results rather than historical results. Accounting profit can be prone to manipulation, unlike share price movements and dividend payments. A further criticism is that an earnings-based measure ignores risk: if a company increases profits by investing in high-risk projects, profits might go up but shareholder value could fall.

(iii) Internal performance measures are measures of performance derived from internal reporting systems, but that are of significance to shareholders. Internal measures can be both financial and non-financial. Financial measures include cash flow return on investment or shareholder value added. Non-financial measures can relate to any key performance objective, such as customer satisfaction (however measured) or the creation of intellectual capital. With the growth in the use of a balanced scorecard approach to setting performance targets, it seems likely that many incentive schemes will be based on internal measures.

(b) A performance measure should follow five basic principles.

(i) It should be clearly linked to the strategic goals of the company.

(ii) A performance measure for an individual should, as far as possible, reflect the contribution of that individual to achieving the performance.

(iii) The performance measure should be identifiable with the interests of shareholders and the wider stakeholder community.

(iv) The measure should require the minimum of adjustment to ensure consistency in the light of strategic and operational changes that occur.

(v) The measure should be proof from manipulation.

(c) The guidelines issued by the ABI have been as follows.

(i) A company's share incentive schemes should be submitted for shareholder approval every five years.

(ii) The granting of share options should be 'little and often' rather than in large amounts and occasionally. This is to avoid the problems that arise when the share price falls soon after options are issued (putting the options 'under water' possibly for a long time) or when the share price is temporarily low and rises substantially soon after the options are issued.

(iii) Performance targets should be demanding and stretching. The ABI has expressed reservations about the desirability of TSR as an incentive measure of performance.

(iv) The ABI supports the concept of a sliding scale of rewards, depending on how the company's performance compares with the performance of other companies over the same period. (This overcomes the problem of rewarding executives for comparatively poor performance , for example, in a period when all share prices rise due to a bull stock market.)

(v) Shareholders should be informed about the likely cost of the incentive scheme before they vote on approving it.

(vi) The ABI also supports incentive plans that encourage executives to build a meaningful shareholding in the company.

(d) Suggestions are as follows. (**Tutorial note:** Three suggestions are given here. Only two are required by the question.)

(i) The remuneration committee could be required to justify their remuneration policy to shareholders annually, and the shareholders should be allowed to vote on it. This measure was adopted by the UK government in 2001, although shareholders vote on the overall remuneration policy, not on the remuneration packages of individual directors. (And any vote is not binding on the remuneration committee.)

(ii) To avoid rewarding failure, incentive schemes should be designed more closely to the guiding principles listed above.

(iii) The rewards for failure are often associated with payments in lieu of notice and for unfair/wrongful dismissal, and perhaps also for the transfer of pension rights. These are basic contractual issues that should be tightened up when executives are first appointed

39 GOVERNANCE AND CONTROLS

(a) Several different issues triggered moves towards systematised corporate governance.

(i) The trend towards global investment has meant that large investment institutions in the US in particular, but also in other countries such as the UK, have been seeking to invest large amounts of capital in companies in other countries. US investors, expecting similar treatment from foreign companies

that they received from US companies, expressed concern about the inadequacy of corporate governance in many countries. Many of their concerns focused on the lack of shareholder rights, or the disregard for minority shareholder rights shown by major shareholders or the boards of foreign companies. The move towards systematised corporate governance still has a long way to go in many countries; however, in issuing its principles of corporate governance, the OECD recognised that the demands and expectations of global investors would have to be met if the trend towards global investment (and efficient capital allocation) is to continue.

(ii) There were serious concerns about the standards of financial reporting. In the late 1980s, there were a number of well-publicised corporate failures, which were unexpected because the financial statements of those companies had not given any indication of their financial problems. This raised questions about the quality of external auditing and the effectiveness of professional auditing standards.

(iii) There were also concerns that many large companies were being run for the benefit of their executive directors and senior managers, and not in the interests of shareholders. For example, there were concerns that acquisitions were sometimes made to increase the size of a company and the power of its chief executive, rather than as a means of adding shareholder value. These concerns raised the question of the conflict of interest between the board of directors and the shareholders. A particular concern was the powerful position of individuals holding the positions of both chairman and chief executive office in their company, and the lack of 'balance' in boards of directors.

(iv) Directors' remuneration also became an issue, for two reasons. There is a widely-held view that executive directors are paid excessive amounts, in terms of basic salary, 'perks' and incentives. Some directors appeared to receive high rewards even when the company performed badly or no differently from the 'average' of other companies. Although investment institutions did not object to high pay for talented executives, they believed that incentive schemes were often badly conceived, and that executives were being rewarded for performance that was not necessarily linked to the benefits provided to shareholders, for example in terms of a higher share price.

(v) Although convictions for insider dealing have been rare, there was a suspicion that some directors might be using their inside knowledge about their company to make a personal gain by dealing in shares in the company. For example, directors might sell a large number of shares just ahead of a profits warning by their company, or buy shares just ahead of a public announcement that might be expected to boost the share price.

(b) In order to issue its statement about the effectiveness of controls, the board of directors must obtain evidence of the existence and effective operation of controls and procedures throughout the group. Due to the decentralised nature of this company and the absence of an internal audit department, the confirmation of this evidence will probably have to come from the senior managers of each operating unit. The senior managers or directors of each operating unit would need to summarise the key internal control procedures, and provide written confirmation on a regular basis that these controls are in place and working well. The main board director responsible for each operating unit, the senior managers or directors of the operating unit and the group finance director will probably need to meet to discuss any confirmations that are given.

The board of the parent company should meet regularly, and adopt a schedule of matters to be considered for decision, so ensuring that it maintains control over strategic, financial, operational and compliance issues. The investigation of these matters will probably be delegated to the audit committee, but the main board retains responsibility.

The audit committee should meet regularly, and its remit should include a review of the group's system of internal controls, based on information obtained from both external sources (the external auditors) and internal sources.

As there is no internal audit department, head office staff (probably accounts staff) should visit operating units regularly, to carry out a financial review. The results of these reviews should be reported back to the finance director and the audit committee. The heads of operational units should also be required to report to the audit committee on the adequacy of their system of internal controls.

The board will also exercise control through its approval of the annual budget and performance targets, and a system of regular performance monitoring and reporting.

(i) **The need for a control environment**

A suitable control environment should be provided by a combination of culture and management style, together with management control mechanisms. The necessary culture should be stimulated by the directors' commitment to quality and competence, and the adoption of ethical and behavioural standards throughout the group. Despite the decentralisation of authority within the group, management control mechanisms should ensure that there are clear lines of responsibility and accountability running throughout the group, that budgeting systems are in place, and that management information systems exist for the provision of performance reports in a timely manner. It is likely that some tasks will be performed centrally at head office, perhaps as the responsibility of the finance director. These would include statutory reporting, tax matters and arranging insurance. Budgetary control processes should be in place and operating properly. Operating units should be given clear and achievable targets aligned with the group's overall objectives, and these targets should be known to the senior management in each operating unit. There will be some delegation of authority to spend, but within clearly stated limits. Spending decisions above a certain level should be the responsibility of the main board. The board is also required to consider each year the need for an internal audit department or unit.

(ii) **Evaluation of risks**

The board should have a focus on the control and containment of risks, based on a cost/benefit approach. Controls are likely to include a board policy not to invest in any operation outside a specific area of 'competence', so that acquisitions are not made that alter the risk profile of the company's businesses. All divisions should have at least one main board director actively involved, so that there is direct knowledge of operating units at main board level. The main board should discuss all major proposed new ventures, and when a new venture is given the go-ahead, it should operate with clear financial constraints. Spending above a certain amount should require full board approval. There should be an information system that reports on performance in a way that non-performing or under-performing units can be identified as soon as possible. New operations and under-performing units should be monitored closely by the board, and the board should have a policy of closing down under-performing units that do not improve. The board should also consider other risks on a regular basis, such as the risk from new technology. The risk of non-compliance with legal and regulatory requirements might be controlled at head office level by the finance director. Insurance arrangements might also be controlled centrally.

In considering the soundness of the system of internal controls, the board should consider the nature and extent of the risks facing the company, the extent and types of risk that it is reasonable for the company to bear, the likelihood of the risks materialising, the ability of the company to minimise the incidence and impact of risks when they do materialise and the costs and benefits of operating particular controls.

(iii) **Information and communication systems**

The group should prepare budgets and budget packs for each operating unit, and budget information should be communicated to senior managers in each unit. The budget should be approved by the main board. There should be regular budget reports comparing actual results against the budget. Managers in each operating unit should be able to extract up-to-date information about the current state of affairs in their unit, from the management information system.

(iv) **Control procedures**

The group should have a range of control procedures in place. The external auditors should check that the financial controls are operating effectively. Controls include specific limits on the authorisation of spending at different levels of management, a suitable segregation of duties in the accounts department, the use of accounting controls (such as bank reconciliations), and suitable controls for computer systems (password controls, physical security for cheque books and computer equipment, etc.)

(v) **Monitoring and corrective action**

There should be regular reports to the main board on internal controls, and the audit committee should be given responsibility for monitoring the control system. The board should also discuss the risk and control implications of major changes, such as new acquisitions. Whenever a weakness or failure in the control system is discovered, corrective action should be taken The finance director should have specific responsibility for explaining to the board any weaknesses or deficiencies uncovered in the system of financial controls.

40 OBJECTIVES AND INCENTIVES

(a) To: Senior non-executive director
From: Financial adviser
Date:

Corporate objectives and incentive schemes

I have been asked to prepare a report on the company's current corporate objective and on the existing incentive schemes in place that are designed to assist with the achievement of the corporate objective.

The current stated corporate objective is the maximisation of shareholder wealth. The concept that the primary financial objective of the firm is to maximise the wealth of shareholders, by which is meant the net present value of estimated future cash flows, underpins much of modern financial theory. The wealth of shareholders can be measured in terms of increases in the value of their shares and dividends received.

According to the theory of share values, investing in profitable projects with a long-term return will increase the current value of the shares, because in an efficient market the future expected benefits will be reflected in the current share price.

However, there is a great deal of difference between long-term performance and short-term performance. It is possible to achieve progress towards an objective in the short term, whilst failing to make progress in the longer term. In the case of this company, this can be seen in the history of the share price over the past five years. In three years, the share price went up and in two years it went down. Overall, the share price increase has been just 15%.

It might therefore be more appropriate to focus on other objectives which, if achieved, should ensure that over the longer term, shareholder wealth will be maximised.

A further problem is that unless the objective of maximising shareholder wealth is consistent with the objectives of other stakeholders in the company, it is unlikely that the other stakeholders will act in a way that contributes toward that objective. The objective of maximising shareholder wealth must be brought into line with the interests of other stakeholder groups.

The **stakeholder view** of corporate objectives is that many groups of people have a stake in what the company does. Each of these groups, which include suppliers, workers, manager, customers and governments as well as shareholders, has its own objectives and interests. The varied interests are likely to be in conflict, unless some way is found to reduce them.

The potential conflict of interest is greatest between the shareholders and the board of directors. The purpose of remuneration schemes should be to try to bring the interests of directors and shareholders into line, but it has clearly failed in the case of this company. The directors have not been particularly successful in maximising shareholder wealth, but have succeeded in obtaining a bonus in three years out of the past five. Judging by the 'pay off' to the operations director, it also seems likely that the directors are protected by terms and conditions in their contract of employment, to an extent that might not be justified.

The interests of senior executives below board level should also be considered, because their efforts are also important for achieving the long-term goal of shareholder wealth maximisation. Similarly, the company should not overlook the interests of the public, who include its customers. If a company acts against the interests of customers and the public, it is quite likely that in the longer term, this will have adverse consequences. If the public stops buying a company's products, for example, profits and shareholder wealth will be eroded.

Perhaps at the initiative of the non-executive directors, the company should consider the following measures.

(i) Re-negotiating the remuneration packages of the executive directors, and trying to develop an incentive scheme for individual directors that rewards them for success, but not failure. A bonus based on share price movements over 12 months is clearly inadequate and unsuitable. There are various ways in which a bonus scheme could be devised, such as a profit-related or EPS-related incentive scheme, or an incentive scheme that rewards directors on their achievement of a number of different financial and non-financial targets.

(ii) The share option scheme should have the effect of linking rewards to the long-term share price performance. The company should consider extending the option scheme to other senior executives. It should also take note of the ABI

recommendation that share options should be issued frequently and in smaller amounts rather than occasionally in large amounts.

(iii) The company should give careful thought to setting objectives for performance that are consistent with long-term success. The poor public image of the company should be a cause for some concern. The board of directors should probably consider setting additional objectives with a customer focus and with a focus on social responsibility.

(iv) The executive directors are responsible for motivating the company's managers and employees, but the non-executives should recognise that their own task is to reduce the potential for a conflict of interest between executive directors and the shareholders. This should be their main immediate concern. If the problem with the directors can be resolved, the directors will be in a better position to deal with managers, employees, customers and the public.

(b) The choice of an appropriate remuneration policy for executives will depend, among other things, on:

(i) Cost: the extent to which the package provides value for money

(ii) Motivation: the extent to which the package motivates employees both to stay with the company and to work to their full potential

(iii) Fiscal effects: government tax incentives may promote different types of pay. At present in the UK there are tax benefits in offering some types of share option schemes. At times of wage control and high taxation this can act as an incentive to make the 'perks' a more significant part of the package

(iv) Goal congruence: the extent to which the package encourages employees to work in such a way as to achieve the objectives of the firm.

In this context, Option (i) is likely to be relatively expensive with no payback to the firm in times of low profitability. It is unlikely to encourage staff to maximise their efforts, although the extent to which it acts as a motivator will depend on the individual psychological make-up of the employees concerned. Many staff prefer this type of package however, since they know where they are financially. In the same way the company is also able to budget accurately for its staff costs.

Provided that the scheme qualifies, the firm will be able to gain fiscal benefits from operating a profit-related pay scheme (Option (ii)). It also benefits from the fact that costs will be lower, though not proportionately so, during a time of low profits. The effect on motivation will vary with the individual concerned, and will also depend on whether it is an individual or a group performance calculation. There is a further risk that figures and performance may be manipulated by managers in such a way as to maximise their bonus to the detriment of the overall longer term company benefit.

A share option scheme (Option (iii)) carries fiscal benefits in the same way as the performance related pay above. It also minimises the cost to the firm since this is effectively borne by the existing shareholders through the dilution of their holdings.

Depending on how pricing is determined, it may assist in achieving goal congruence. However, since the share price depends on many factors which are external to the firm, it is possible for the scheme to operate in a way which is unrelated to the individual's performance. Thus such a scheme is unlikely to motivate directly through links with performance. Staff will continue to obtain the vast majority of their income from salary and perks and are thus likely to be more concerned with maximising these elements of their income than with working to raise the share price.

recommendation that senior managers should be rewarded on the [illegible] rather than concentrating on short term results.

(iii) The committee should give careful thought to [illegible] for [illegible] and [illegible] which is [illegible] success. The [illegible] should be [illegible] to [illegible] the [illegible] with [illegible] and with a focus on [illegible] growth.

(iv) The executive directors are responsible for motivating the company's managers and employees, but the non-executives should recognise that their own task is to reduce the potential for a conflict of interest between executive directors and the shareholder. This should be [illegible]. If the problem with the directors can be resolved the directors will be in a better position to deal with managers, employees, customers and the public.

(b) The choice of an appropriate remuneration package for executives will depend, among other things, on:

(i) [illegible] the extent to which the package provides value for money;

(ii) [illegible] the extent to which the package [illegible] employees to [illegible] the company and to work to their full potential;

(iii) [illegible] share option [illegible] employees may [illegible] different types of [illegible]. At times of [illegible] and high taxation [illegible] can be [illegible] the [illegible] of the [illegible];

(iv) [illegible] whether [illegible] the [illegible] of [illegible] employees to work [illegible] as [illegible] the [illegible] of the firm.

In this case, option (b) is likely to be [illegible] with [illegible]. The [illegible] with [illegible] the extent to which it is [illegible] will depend on the individual psychological make-up of the employees concerned. Many staff [illegible] that [illegible] since they [illegible] where they are [illegible]. In the [illegible] is also able to [illegible] accurately the overall cost.

[illegible] the scheme [illegible] option (c) will be able to [illegible]. Option (c) is also [illegible] from the fact that costs will be lower [illegible]. The effect on motivation will vary with the individual concerned and will also depend on whether it is an individual or group performance calculation. There is a further risk that figures [illegible] may be manipulated by [illegible] in such a way as to maximise their bonus to the detriment of the overall longer term company position.

A share option scheme (option (d)) carries [illegible] in the same way as the performance related pay above. It also [illegible] the [illegible] to the [illegible] that it is [illegible] closely [illegible] by the existing shareholders through the [illegible] of [illegible] returns.

Depending on how pricing is determined, it may [illegible] and [illegible]. However, since the share price depends on many factors which are external to the firm and outside the [illegible] in a way which [illegible] the individual performance of [illegible], such a scheme is unlikely to [illegible] staff [illegible]. Staff will continue to [illegible] and [illegible] are [illegible] likely to be more concerned with [illegible] income than with [illegible] to [illegible] the share [illegible].

Mock exam questions

Note:

In the Module B exam, Subject Area 4 on Risk Management is combined with Subject Area 3, Financial Strategy.

The whole three hour exam would consist of:

Section A: 20 MCQs, 10 on each subject area

Section B: 3 written questions on Subject Area 3

Section C: 3 written questions on Subject Area 4

You are required to answer all of Section A, one question from each of Sections B and C, and one further question from either Section B **or** Section C.

To do this mock exam on Subject Area 4, you should allow yourself the following timings:

Section A – 36 minutes

Section C – 36 minutes for each 20 mark question you attempt

SECTION A - ANSWER ALL THE QUESTIONS

1 What does the term matching refer to?

A A mechanism whereby a company balances its foreign currency inflows and outflows
B The coupling of two simple financial instruments to create a more complex one
C The adjustment of credit terms between companies
D Contracts not yet offset by futures contracts or fulfilled by delivery

2 Calculate the forward per annum premium or discount given the following information:

Spot £1 = $1.4000; 3 month forward £1 = $1.4200

A The $ is at a premium of 1.43 percent
B The $ is at a discount of 1.43 percent
C The $ is at a premium of 5.71 percent
D The $ is at a discount of 5.71 percent

3 What is the correct definition of value at risk?

A A single number estimate of how much a company can lose due to the price volatility of the instrument held

B The standard deviation of the changes in value of the total portfolio of instruments held by a company

C The variability of movements in a security's price

D The total amount of interest payable as a percentage of the amount lent or borrowed.

4 A firm deals a $5 Million 3 v 6 FRA on 8 April 2001 for settlement on 8 July 2001, based on a maturity date of 8 October 2001. The contract period is 90 days and the contract rate is 9.05%. The three-month LIBOR fixing is 9.5%. Given the above information, what would be the amount payable to the buyer on 8 July 2001?

A $ 5,500.55
B $ 10,762.98
C $ 5,494.51
D $ 10,739.86

5 To what does interest rate risk relate?

A The sensitivity of profit, cash flow or valuation of the firm to fluctuations in the interest rate

B The difference between short term interest rates prevailing in two money centres at any given time

C Futures contracts which relate wholly to levels of interest rates

D The condition that the interest differential should equal the forward differential between two currencies

6 What is the expected rate of return on a share with a β of 1.5, where the risk free rate is 6% and the market risk premium is 8.6%?

A 9.9%
B 12.5%
C 21.5%
D 18.9%

7 Which of the following statements is true?

A A high interest rate positively affects the value of a put option
B A high interest rate adversely affects the value of a put option
C Volatility of the underlying share decreases the value of a put option
D The market price of a put option increases as the share price increases

8 Which of the following is **NOT** a recommended structure for good governance?

A Audit Committee
B Employee Representative
C The Board
D Remuneration Committee

9 Using the following information, which of the variables is the least sensitive with regard to the overall profitability of the project?

Initial costs = £15,000 ; Ongoing costs = £2,000 p.a. ; Revenue = £5,000 p.a. ; Project life 8 years.

A Initial Costs
B Ongoing Costs
C Revenue
D Project Life

10 A UK company is bidding for a contract with the Thai government, but will not know for three months if the bid has been accepted. The company will need Thai currency (the Thai Bhat) to cover expenses but will be paid in sterling by the Thai Government if it is awarded the contract. In order to minimise its exposure to currency risk, what should the UK company do?

A Sell Thai Bhat futures
B Buy Thai Bhat futures
C Buy Thai Bhat put option
D Buy Thai Bhat call options

> **Note:** In the whole module B examination, Section B would consist of 3 20 mark questions on Financial Strategy (subject area 3) and Section C would consist of the three questions on Risk Management. Candidates must answer one question from each of Section B and C, and one other question which can be taken from either section.

SECTION C

11 Financial Reporting Standard 3 (FRS3) states, 'It is not possible to distil the performance of a complex organisation into a single measure'. Nevertheless, the 'Principles of Good Governance' as espoused in the 'Combined Code' highlight many instances where information of this nature is key to the implementation of good governance.

Required:

(a) Outline the range of metrics available to measure corporate performance. (8 marks)

(b) What principles should be followed in establishing a performance measure and how could such performance information be used in the implementation of good governance ? (12 marks)

(20 marks)

12 (a) Discuss the factors that may impact on a company's policy on the payment of dividends. (10 marks)

(b) Assuming that a company wishes to maximise shareholder wealth, what are the arguments for and against each of the following approaches?

(i) payment of a low but constant dividend per share, with regular scrip issues and shareholder incentives

(ii) payment of no dividends to shareholders

(iii) consistent payment of 50% of earnings after tax as dividend (10 marks)

(20 marks)

13 Hyndland PLC produces a range of domestic plastic products. The company is considering expanding its market and entering into the industrial moulded plastics market, specifically supplying moulded plastic body parts for motor cars.

The risk free rate of return is currently 7% and the company can borrow at 2% over this. The market risk premium is estimated at 9% and the corporate tax burden is 22% p.a. Hyndlands' $\alpha = 1.25\%$.

Selected financial data concerning four of Hyndland's competitors in the domestic plastics products markets are given below:

	Hyndland	*Barrowfield*	*Carmyle*	*Wells*	*Toddy*
	£'000	£'000	£'000	£'000	£'000
Fixed assets	25,600	19,800	29,600	33,100	17,500
Working capital	17,700	14,600	12,200	16,100	14,600
	43,300	34,400	41,800	49,200	32,100
Bank loans	22,400	10,300	17,600	23,200	9,000
Ordinary shares	9,000	9,000	14,000	8,500	10,300
Reserves	16,900	20,100	15,200	22,800	17,800
	48,300	39,400	46,800	54,500	37,100
Turnover	50,000	40,200	47,700	52,300	33,400
EPS	1.045	0.30	0.473	0.35	0.33
Div / Share	40p	11p	20p	15p	14p
P/E Ratio	08:01	12:01	10:01	09:01	14:01
Beta (equity)	0.5	1.3	1.5	1.1	1.05
Nominal share value	0.5	0.25	0.5	0.25	1

Required:

Assuming that corporate debt may be assumed to be effectively risk free;

(a) Explain the meaning and significance of Hyndland's α and equity β values. (5 marks)

(b) Estimate the discount rate Hyndland should use in assessing the risk of its suggested expansion into the industrial moulded plastics market. (10 marks)

(c) Discuss the differences in the cost of debt and equity. (5 marks)

(20 marks)

Mock exam answers

1 C Option A is a definition of matching
Option C is a definition of simple financial engineering
Option D is a definition of open interest

2 D $\frac{1.42 - 1.4}{1.4} \times \frac{12}{3} \times 100$

Option A $\frac{1.42 - 1.4}{1.4} \times 100$: misses out the annualisation
Option B misses out the annualisation but is quoted as a discount
Option C misses out annualisation but is quoted as a premium

3 A Option B is part of the mechanism for calculating the VaR
Option C is a definition of volatility
Option D is a definition of yield

4 C $\$5{,}494.51 = \frac{(0.095 - 0.0905) \times 5{,}000{,}000 \times 90/360}{1 + (0.095 \times 90/360)}$

Option A: $\$5{,}500.55 = \frac{(0.095 - 0.0905) \times 5{,}000{,}000 \times 90/360}{1 + (0.0905 \times 90/360)}$

Option B: $\$10{,}762.98 = \frac{(0.095 - 0.0905) \times 5{,}000{,}000 \times 90/180}{1 + (0.0905 \times 90/180)}$

Option D: $\$10{,}739.86 = \frac{(0.095 - 0.0905) \times 5{,}000{,}000 \times 90/180}{1 + (0.0905 \times 90/180)}$

5 A Option B is a definition of interest rate spread
Option C is a definition of interest rate futures
Option D is a definition of interest rate parity

6 D 18.9% = 6% + (1.5 × 8.6%)

Option A: 9.9% = 6% + 1.5 (8.6% – 6%)
Option B: 12.5% = 8.6% + 1.5 (8.6% – 6%)
Option C: 21.5% = 8.6% + (1.5 × 8.6%)

7 B All the others are antithetical.

8 B

9 A (60%)

Option B: 56.25%
Option C: 22.5%
Option D: 37.5%

10 D

11 (a)

> **Tutorial note.** The term 'metrics' is management-speak. It is derived from the metric system (i.e. measurement system based on metres), and means a system or basis of measurement.

The performance of a complex organisation is difficult to assess with a single measure. Performance measures should ideally relate to a number of different objectives of the organisation, and should consider the longer-term as well as the short-term. The effect of performance on future prospects is possibly more important than the effect on historical results. Performance can be measured in non-financial terms as well as financially. Various measures can be used to measure the performance of individual business units, but these would not be appropriate for measuring the performance of the organisation as a whole.

The question refers to matters of corporate governance. The key issue for corporate governance is that senior management should have some incentive to work towards achieving results for their company that meet the overall objectives of the company. An incentive system should be designed so as to overcome the potential conflict of interest between shareholders and directors, and between the directors and other stakeholders in the company. The incentive system needs to be simple and clearly understood; however, there is a risk that the performance target or targets selected will not encourage senior managers to try to achieve results that are in the long-term best interests of shareholders. For example, rewarding managers on the achievement of profit targets could encourage short-term decision-making at the expense of longer-term considerations.

Measures of overall company performance can be grouped into three broad categories, market-based measures, earnings-based measures and internal measures.

Market-based measures are used to judge performance of the company on the basis of changes in the market value of the company's shares. An increase in the share price reflects the creation of shareholder value, and so could be seen as directly linked to the overall objective of the organisation. A market-based performance measure should, however, allow for dividends paid to shareholders, since dividends represent value added for shareholders paid out by the company. Examples of market-based measures are market value added (MVA) and total shareholder return (TSR). However, given the fact that share prices continually fluctuate, and that the share price will also be affected by market sentiment, there are limitations to the reliability of measuring performance simply by means of changes in the share value between two points in time. The ABI recommends that where TSR is used as a performance measure, at least one other performance measure should be used as well.

Earnings-based measures of performance focus on profitability, and commonly-used measures are earnings per share and growth in EPS, and return on investment (ROI). Although widely-used, earnings-based measures suffer from several drawbacks. They are based on historical performance, and give no consideration to the effect of performance by management on the future of the company. They also ignore risk. Management can increase earnings by investing in projects with a higher risk profile: and so change the risk characteristics of the business. This will affect shareholders' views of risk premium, and so investments that add to profits could actually destroy shareholder value. Profit measurements are also notoriously subject to manipulation by management, despite efforts by the Accounting Standards Board to prevent 'window dressing' in accounts.

Internal measures of performance are measures that are compared with an internal benchmark or target, rather than being based on external comparisons. Internal measures can be financial or non-financial. Financial measures include shareholder added value and cash flow return on investment. Non-financial measures might be based on targets relating to customer satisfaction, innovation, modernisation/productivity gains or the development of intellectual capital within the company. A balanced scorecard to performance measurements reflects an appreciation that measuring corporate performance calls for the consideration of several targets, both financial and non-financial.

Measuring corporate performance and remunerating senior executives on the basis of that performance remains a highly contentious issue in corporate governance. The problem remains that an incentive remuneration scheme needs to focus on just one or a small number of targets, whereas the actual performance of a complex organisation cannot be easily distilled into a small handful of measures.

(b) The Combined Code states that the board of directors has a general responsibility to present a balanced and understandable assessment of the company's position and prospects.

A measure of performance should be established on the following principles.

(i) It should be consistent with the strategic goals of the organisation, and should be clearly linked to the achievement of those objectives.

(ii) It should monitor the performance of the individual who is being assessed, and should reflect the achievements of that individual.

(iii) It should be identifiable with the interests of the company's shareholders, and with the interests of other stakeholders on the company.

(iv) It should be robust, in the sense that it should not need to be changed substantially to provide consistency in performance assessment whenever structural or operational changes affect the company.

(v) It should not be prone to manipulation by management, particularly the manager whose performance is being judged.

Performance measures are an important element of good corporate governance.

(i) As indicated above, performance measures should be used as a basis for incentive-based remuneration of senior executives. A well-designed incentive system can motivate senior executives to work towards corporate performance that is in the best interests of shareholders and consistent with the interests of other stakeholders in the company.

(ii) Performance measures can also help the board of directors to present a balanced and understandable assessment of the company's position and prospects, by providing further information in addition to that required by statute, regulation or accounting standards. Such information can be presented in the company's published report and accounts, perhaps as part of the operational and financial review.

(iii) An important element of good corporate governance, recognised by the Combined code and OECD principles, is the relationship between the board of directors and the shareholders. Providing information about performance will help to create a meaningful dialogue with shareholders.

12 (a) According to the theory put forward by Modigliani and Miller, dividend policy should be irrelevant to shareholders, because shareholders can make their own adjustments (buying or selling shares) to achieve the level of income they require from their investments.

In practice, however, dividend policy is significant to shareholders. Unexpected changes in dividend payments will have an effect on the share price, and to avoid upsetting the market, a company might try to apply a policy of a consistent payout ratio (ratio of dividends to distributable profits for the year). Companies will often also 'smooth' dividend payments, ignoring 'temporary' fluctuations in annual profitability. Shareholders might therefore expect to receive dividends from a company that grow each year. Market expectations can therefore be a major factor in the formulation of dividend policy, and companies might be extremely reluctant to decide on a dividend cut, even when annual profits are falling.

There are also other factors that affect dividend policy.

(i) The purpose of retaining profits should usually be to invest in new projects, in order to develop and grow the business. Unless there are profitable investments available to invest in, there should be no reason to retain the profits instead of paying them out as dividends.

(ii) Companies are prevented by law from distributing dividends in excess of the distributable reserves of the company. Broadly speaking, distributable profits are cumulative retained profits. A loss-making company might therefore find its ability to pay dividends is restricted.

(iii) Dividends have to be paid in cash (given that scrip dividends are uncommon). In order to make a dividend payment, a company must therefore have sufficient free cash flow to afford to make the payment. It is quite possible for a company to make profits but have insufficient cash to pay a suitable dividend.

(iv) Dividend policy could also be affected by the availability of new finance, particularly debt capital. A company needing capital to invest could decide to pay out a high dividend, and to borrow the money it needs for investment. In effect, this dividend policy would also be a policy of increasing the financial gearing ratio.

(v) The board of directors might want to use dividend policy to provide signals to the market about expectations for future profits and growth. An increase in dividends could be used to signal optimism about the future. If the signal is well-received, the share price could be boosted.

(vi) In the case of private companies where most of the shares are owned by a small number of individuals, dividend policy might be determined by the tax position of the individual shareholders. If the shareholder-directors wish to avoid paying income tax, they can retain profits in the company instead of paying them out as dividends.

(b) Each of the three dividend policies could be attractive to a particular type of investor.

(i) A policy of paying a low dividend, and retaining a high proportion of profits, might be pursued by a company that is investing in future growth, and prefers retained profits to raising new capital to provide the capital for investment. The payment of some dividend would attract shareholders looking for a predictable and sustainable dividend income stream. However, the shareholders would also expect annual dividend growth, to justify the retention and reinvestment of such a large proportion of profits. The regular payment of scrip dividends would make little sense for a private company, but could be of some benefit for shareholders in a company whose shares are traded on a stock market. Receiving new shares could, arguably, give them more flexibility in their investment choices. If a shareholder prefers cash to new shares, he can simply sell the shares received as dividend (although his shareholding in the company, as a percentage of the total shares in issue, would decline). Other shareholder incentives presumably mean various 'perks' that are offered by some companies, such as cut-price tickets or rooms offered to shareholders by some transport companies and hotel chains. These are not dividends, and have no relevance to dividend policy.

(ii) A policy of paying no dividends at all, at least in the short term, should be pursued by a company aiming at re-investing to achieve profit growth. This would be of no appeal to shareholders looking for stable dividend income, but could appeal to investors who are seeking capital growth rather than regular income. Retaining all profits would minimise the need for the company to go to the markets to raise new capital for investment.

(iii) As suggested earlier, shareholders often want a company to have a policy of stable and predictable dividends. A policy of paying 50% of earnings as dividends each year does not necessarily provide this. Annual profits can fluctuate, and if profits go down from one year to the next, a strict 50% payout policy would mean that dividends must be cut as well. A board of directors is often unwilling to cut dividends, even when profits fall, because of the adverse effect this could have on market sentiment and the share price. If dividends are difficult to predict, the share price might be lower than it would otherwise be with a policy of 'smoothing' annual dividends, due to the greater uncertainty for investors. To pay out 50% of profits as dividends would also mean that the company must have sufficient free cash flow to make the payments, and the business must therefore be strongly cash-generative. A large payout ratio would also suggest that the company has little need for new capital to reinvest, and might therefore be appropriate to a company in a 'mature business'.

Whatever dividend policy a company adopts, it would be advisable to make the policy known to investors, so that they can make appropriate investment decisions.

13 (a) An alpha value is a measurement of the amount by which the actual returns achieved for a specific share (or portfolio of shares) is greater or less than the expected return, given the systematic risk associated with the share and the excess of the expected market return over the risk-free rate. A positive alpha value shows that the return on the share was higher than would have been expected, whereas a negative alpha value indicates a lower-than-expected return. If the alpha value is negative, shareholders might be expected to sell their shares, until the price falls to a level where the alpha value has risen to zero. Similarly, when the alpha value is positive, investors might be expected to buy the shares until the price rises to a level where the alpha value has been reduced to zero. Hyndland shares have a positive alpha value, suggesting that the share price might soon rise with investor demand to buy the shares.

A beta value for a share (or portfolio of shares) relates to systematic risk or market risk. It is a measure of the sensitivity or volatility of the expected returns on the share to changes in the market and in average market returns. Hyndland shares have a beta of 0.5, which means that if average market returns went up by 1%, the expected returns on Hyndland shares would rise by 0.5 x 1%, i.e. by 0.5%. If returns were measured purely by movements in the share price, this would mean that the Hyndland share price should rise by 0.5%. Systematic risk, unlike unsystematic risk, cannot be eliminated by diversification, because it affects all company shares, even though the scale of systematic risk varies between companies.

(b) Since the company is planning to enter a new market with significantly different risk characteristics (as shown by the differences in equity betas), it would be inappropriate to use its existing cost of capital as a discount rate. It would be more appropriate to estimate a suitable discount rate, using data relating to the competitor companies.

We need to establish an equity beta for the industry. One approach is to take a simple average of the equity betas of the other 4 companies.

> **Tutorial note.** You could take a different approach here, for example by calculating a market-weighted average industry beta.

Industry equity beta = (1.3 + 1.5 + 1.1 + 1.05)/4 = 1.2375, say 1.24.

Using all four competitor companies, we need to calculate the market value of their debt and of their equity. The corporate debt is assumed to be risk-free, so that its market value equals its face value. The market value of equity is the number of shares in issue multiplied by the EPS and the P/E ratio.

		Equity	*Debt*
		£000	£000
Barrowfield	(9,000 × 1/0.25 × £0.30 × 12)	129,600	10,300
Carmyle	(14,000 × 1/0.5 × £0.473 × 10)	132,440	17,600
Wells	(8,500 × 1/0.25 × £0.35 × 9)	107,100	23,200
Toddy	(10,300 × 1 × £0.33 × 14)	47,586	9,000
Total		416,726	60,100
Hyndland	(9,000 × 1/0.5 × £1.045 × 8)	150,480	22,400

The geared beta for the industry is 1.24.

Ungearing this, we get an ungeared beta of:

$$\frac{1.24}{\left[1 + \dfrac{60{,}100\,(1-0.22)}{416{,}726}\right]}$$

= 1.1146.

This ungeared beta can now be converted to a geared beta for Hyndland, using the company's own gearing ratio.

$$\text{Beta} = 1.1146 + 1.1146\left[\frac{22{,}400\,(1-0.22)}{150{,}480}\right]$$

= 1.244.

By chance, this happens to be similar to the average industry beta, as the gearing ratio of Hyndland is similar to that of the industry company average.

Using the CAPM, the cost of Hyndland equity is: 7% + (1.244 × 9%) = 18.196%, say 18.2% or 0.182.

Cost of capital to use:

	Market value £000	Cost	*MV x Cost*
Equity	150,480	0.182	27,387
Debt	22,400	0.09 × (1 – 0.22) = 0.070	1,568
	172,880		28,955

Discount rate to use = 22,955/172,880 = 0.1675, i.e. 16.75% (possibly rounded up to 17%).

(c) The cost of equity should be higher than the cost of debt. The cost of debt is the return payable to debt holders in the form of interest. The cost of equity, on the other hand, is the return expected by shareholders, in the form of dividends and share price growth.

(i) Equity capital has a higher risk for the investor than debt. This is because a company must pay its obligations to lenders before it can make any payments of dividends to shareholders. Returns on debt capital are also predictable, whereas returns to equity shareholders depend on changes in profits and the gearing level. To compensate them for the higher risk associated with holding equity, shareholders should expect higher returns on their investment.

(ii) Companies obtain tax relief on debt interest, but do not get tax relief on dividend payments. The cost of debt should be calculated allowing for the tax relief. For example, if interest on debt is 10% but the rate of corporation tax is 30%, the after-tax cost of debt is only 7%.

The cost of both debt and equity can rise to very high levels, however, when the gearing level becomes high.

ORDER FORM

To order your ACCADipFM books, you can phone us on 020 8740 2211, email us at *publishing@bpp.com*, fax us on 020 8740 1184, or cut out this form and post it to us at the address below.

To: BPP Publishing Ltd, Aldine House, Aldine Place London W12 8AW

Tel: 020 8740 2211
Fax: 020 8740 1184

Forenames (Mr / Ms): ____________________ Surname: ______________________

Daytime delivery address: ____

____

Post code: ______________ Date of exam (month/year):____________________

	Price (£) 6/01 Text	Price (£) 8/01 Kit	Quantity Text	Quantity Kit	Total £
	£	£			
Module A					
Subject area 1: Interpretation of financial statements	39.95	19.95			
Subject area 2: Performance management	39.95	19.95			
Home Study Package *	120.00				
Module B					
Subject area 3: Financial strategy	39.95	19.95			
Subject area 4: Risk management (12/01)	39.95	19.95			
Home Study Package *	120.00				
* Comprises Study Text, Kit, four marked exams plus					
tutorial support					
Project Text ** (12/01)	39.95				
**Guidance on tackling the compulsory project					
component of each module.					
Postage and packaging:					
UK: Texts £3.00 for first plus £2.00 for each extra					
Kits £2.00 for first plus £1.00 for each extra					
Europe (inc ROI): Texts £5.00 for first plus £4.00 for each extra					
Kits £2.50 for first plus £1.00 for each extra					
Rest of the World: Texts £20.00 for first plus £10.00 for each extra					
Kits £15.00 for first plus £8.00 for each extra					
				Total	

We aim to deliver to all UK addresses inside 5 working days; a signature will be required. Orders to all EU addresses should be delivered within 6 working days. All other orders to overseas addresses should be delivered within 8 working days.

I enclose a cheque for £ __________ or charge to Access/Visa/Switch

Card number | | | | | | | | | | | | | | | | | | | |

Start date (Switch only) __________ **Expiry date** ______________ **Issue no. (Switch only)**___

Signature ________________________

REVIEW FORM & FREE PRIZE DRAW

All original review forms from the entire BPP range, completed with genuine comments, will be entered into one of two draws on 31 July 2002 and 31 January 2003. The names on the first four forms picked out on each occasion will be sent a cheque for £50.

Name: ______________________ **Address:** ______________________

____

Date: ______________________ ______________________

How have you used this Practice & Revision Kit?
(Tick one box only)

- ☐ Home study (book only)
- ☐ On a course: college ______________
- ☐ With 'correspondence' package
- ☐ Other ______________

Why did you decide to purchase this Practice & Revision Kit? *(Tick one box only)*

- ☐ Have used complementary Textbook
- ☐ Have used BPP Texts in the past
- ☐ Recommendation by friend/colleague
- ☐ Recommendation by a lecturer at college
- ☐ Saw advertising
- ☐ Other ______________

During the past six months do you recall seeing/receiving any of the following?
(Tick as many boxes as are relevant)

- ☐ Our advertisement in *ACCA Diploma Newsletter*
- ☐ Other advertisement ______________
- ☐ Our brochure with a letter through the post

Which (if any) aspects of our advertising do you find useful?
(Tick as many boxes as are relevant)

- ☐ Prices and publication dates of new editions
- ☐ Information on Practice & Revision Kit content
- ☐ Facility to order books off-the-page
- ☐ None of the above

Have you used the companion textbook for this subject? ☐ Yes ☐ No

Your ratings, comments and suggestions would be appreciated on the following areas

	Very useful	*Useful*	*Not useful*
Introductory section (How to use this Practice & Revision Kit)	☐	☐	☐
Multiple choice question bank	☐	☐	☐
Practice questions	☐	☐	☐
Answer banks	☐	☐	☐
Mock exam	☐	☐	☐
Structure & presentation	☐	☐	☐

	Excellent	*Good*	*Adequate*	*Poor*
Overall opinion of this Kit	☐	☐	☐	☐

Do you intend to continue using BPP Interactive Texts/Kits? ☐ Yes ☐ No

Please note any further comments and suggestions/errors on the reverse of this page.

Please return to: Pippa Riley, BPP Publishing Ltd, FREEPOST, London, W12 8BR

REVIEW FORM & FREE PRIZE DRAW (continued)

Please note any further comments and suggestions/errors below

FREE PRIZE DRAW RULES

1 Closing date for 31 July 2002 draw is 30 June 2002. Closing date for 31 January 2003 draw is 31 December 2002.

2 Restricted to entries with UK and Eire addresses only. BPP employees, their families and business associates are excluded.

3 No purchase necessary. Entry forms are available upon request from BPP Publishing. No more than one entry per title, per person. Draw restricted to persons aged 16 and over.

4 Winners will be notified by post and receive their cheques not later than 6 weeks after the relevant draw date.

5 The decision of the promoter in all matters is final and binding. No correspondence will be entered into.